A THAOISIGH

an open letter to a callous politician and others

The story of the richest Government in the European Union's continuing complicity in and neglect and indifference to the plight of an Irish family and the Irish Government's continuing support for a self-admitted sexual deviant.

Máire & Seán Ó L........

CARRAIG PRESS

© Máire & Seán Ó L 2007

All rights reserved.

No part of this publication may be reproduced, copied or transmitted in any form, or by any means, without the written permission of the publishers, other than by way of *bona fide* review and media purposes.

A catalogue record is available for this book from the National Library of Ireland and the British Library.

ISBN: 978-0-9557827-0-1

First published 2007 by
CARRAIG PRESS
1 Doonanore Park,
Dún Laoghaire,
Co. Dublin
Tel: +353 1 285 2398
email: carraigpress@gmail.com

A Thaoisigh

To our two heroines, S. and D., to whose welfare all our efforts are directed with love.

To all our family, friends and neighbours, who have supported us so magnificently in both Ireland and Australia.

To thousands and thousands of our children, including S., who are deprived and neglected by the richest Government in the European Union.

To the parents of Ireland who should be alert and circumspect to any proposals of this Government to curtail their existing rights under Bunreacht na hÉireann.

To the journalists and their editors of Ireland and Australia who not only keep us informed but sane and sometimes amused and sometimes vexed.

To Rosa Parks who made a difference to her and to our world.

To all who work in the care of children and especially to Dr. Bill Glaser in acknowledgement of and gratitude for his immense work in the field of paedophilia, which he more correctly terms *child sexual assault*.

To God who has given us the strength to survive and to write.

Saeva ignatio ulterius cor lacerare nequit. Abi, lector, et imitare, si poteris, strenuum pro virili libertatis vindicatorem.

Savage indignation can no longer lacerate his heart. Go, reader, and imitate if you can one who with all his might championed liberty.

Ní féidir leis an bhfearg fíochmhar a chroí a lascadh a thuilleadh. Imigh, a léitheoir, agus déan aithris ar dhuine a sheas ceart don saoirse.

Mr. Bertie Ahern, T.D., 30th August 2007
An Taoiseach.

A Thaoisigh,

Imagine a society afflicted by a scourge which struck down a quarter of its daughters and up to one in eight of its sons. Imagine also that this plague, while not immediately fatal, lurked in the bodies and minds of these young children for decades, making them up to sixteen times more likely to experience its disastrous long-term effects. Finally, imagine the nature of these effects: life-threatening starvation, suicide, persistent nightmares, drug and alcohol abuse and a whole host of intractable psychiatric disorders requiring life-long treatment. What should that society's response be?

The scourge that we are speaking of is child sexual abuse. It has accounted for probably more misery and suffering than any of the great plagues of history, including the bubonic plague, tuberculosis and syphilis. Its effects are certainly more devastating and widespread than those of the modern-day epidemics which currently take up so much community attention and resources: motor vehicle accidents, heart disease and, now, AIDS. Yet the public response to child sexual abuse, even now, is fragmented, poorly coordinated and generally ill-informed. Its victims have no National AIDS Council to advise governments on policy and research issues. They have no National Heart Foundation to promote public education as to the risks of smoking and unhealthy lifestyles. They do not have a Transport Accident Commission to provide comprehensive treatment and rehabilitation services for them.

A massive public health problem like child sexual abuse demands a massive societal response. But firstly, we need to acknowledge and understand the problem itself, and this is, sadly enough, a task which both professionals and the community have been reluctant to undertake, despite the glaringly obvious evidence in front of us.

These are not our words. They are the opening remarks of Dr. Bill Glaser, Honorary Senior Lecturer in the Department of Psychiatry at the University of Melbourne and Consultant Psychiatrist to the sex offender treatment programme of the Forensic Psychiatric Services of the Human Services Department of Victoria. He was addressing a specific conference organised by the Australian Institute of Criminology on the theme of Paedophilia / Policy and / Prevention in April 1997.

In line with both professionals and the community we too *have been reluctant to undertake, despite the glaringly obvious evidence in front of us,* publicly this task, *to acknowledge and understand the problem,* having foolishly thought that over two and a half years of dealing privately with you and your Government would not require us to do so. In addition to Dr. Glaser's exhortation, Christ himself encourages us through three of his evangelists, Matthew, Mark and your friend Luke twice *For there is nothing hidden that will not be disclosed and nothing concealed that will not be known or brought out into the open* (Lk. 8.17) and again *There is nothing concealed that will not be disclosed or hidden that will not be made known* (Lk. 12.2).

How could you, a Thaoisigh, so ignore our beautiful grand-daughter, S., her innocent mother, D., and this Teaghlach as to allow S., aged five, to be brought by legal requirement from our home to Sydney Airport, there to be handed over at the Airport to a bi-sexual predator who has been sexually abusing her since she was only three years old, and to remain with him unsupervised for three weeks?

You, Bertie Ahern, of all Taoisigh, a father of two girls, the first Taoiseach ever and probably the first Government leader ever to come to power on the back of paedophilia, how could you chose to ignore our pleas, entreaties and harrowing suffering since January 2005?

So, now, we address this open letter to you and your Government. Please read and heed us this time and respond with the protection that is our right. No more prevarication, a Thaoisigh. No more passing the parcel about the Cabinet table as though our beautiful now six-year-old grand-daughter was nothing more than a

Government plaything. No more ignoring of her and our rights as Irish citizens. No more treating us as less than human, unworthy of either your time or interest. No more acting as though Bunreacht na hÉireann doesn't exist or at least does not apply to the Fianna Fáil and Progressive Democrat parties, particularly each and every one of their members in Government.

We are one in a million. Indeed, as we write to a chartered accountant let us be fully accurate: we are one in 1.053 million. The 2007 Census tells us so, 1,053,000 families, each individual and unique yet interlinked in the core values of kinship, neighbourliness and friendship. *Ar scáth a chéile a mhaireann na daoine* or as John Donne reminds us, *No man is an island, entire of itself; every man is a piece of the continent, a part of the main.*

That is us. One in 1.053 million. You don't know us, never met us, chose not to meet us. You should have, could have, but chose not to. In a population of 4,239,848 people 1.053 million families is a lot of people to ignore, to choose to ignore. What you've done to one you've done to all. Shame on you. It was your choice.

Like the vast majority of Irish families we lived quietly, out of the spotlight, raising our children, paying our mortgages and our taxes, funding our Governments of whatever political persuasion and being the base that gave life to the famous Celtic Tiger of the nineties. Without our hard work, our taxes, our children, the Celtic Tiger could never have been born. 1.053 million families each with its own story, most not wishing to tell. Just like us – until events and most of all a callous Taoiseach leave us with no other option.

Again like the vast majority of Irish families we never asked anything extra of our politicians or our Government through our 129 years of citizenship. Until of course we encountered our current problems and became even more horrified to come to know of and suffer the complicity, duplicity, inefficiency and heartlessness of our own Government and your administration. It is over two years and seven months since we first raised matters of S. and D. with An Roinn Gnóthaí Eachtracha, the Department of Foreign Affairs. 945 days. 22,320 hours. 1,350,800 minutes. And you, Bertie, the man of the people, couldn't, didn't, chose not to give us even thirty, twenty or ten of those 1.35 million minutes. No one knows better than yourself how many of those minutes you frittered away including demeaning your great office by taking it to open a beauty salon of your erstwhile lover in Limerick and the interminable time you and your Government colleagues devote to the tawdry shenanigans of your personal finances. But then how could the life and abuse of a three and a half now six year old girl compare to such lofty matters of State?

As a father of two daughters you are well aware that little girls of three and a half do not go away. They grow into bigger girls of six as S. is now and into teenagers and young women, carrying their memories into adulthood. As our Courts more and more testify to, where those memories are of abuse whether sexual or physical those young lives continue to be scarred if not destroyed by those memories. And you chose not to listen. How callous, how heartless. As the only leader of a political party that we know of who came to power on the back of paedophilia we would have confidently expected understanding and action from you. Nor unlike in that case when the availability of a particular file remains a bone of contention between your predecessor and yourself you cannot deny knowledge of S.'s, D.'s or our case. We have assiduously kept An Roinn Gnóthaí Eachtracha and yourself informed of every twist and turn in our affairs since they first surfaced in January 2005.

As Taoiseach you more than any other Taoiseach have had to focus and deal with the canker of paedophilia and child pornography across so many sections of our society infecting our churches, our schools, our sports and such institutions of State as the judiciary and the State Solicitor's office. How close to Government is that? Yet you and your Government and your administration can be complicit in and stand with and support such canker in our family, while standing four-square with the perpetrator against S., D. and us. Umpteen times we have written to you, delivering our letters by hand or by registered post, copying them to each member of Government and to the Minister of State for Children who sits at the Cabinet table for we, even if Ministers don't, believe in Cabinet responsibility, and finally, Bertie, sending a copy to you at your constituency office, St. Luke's, and to Uachtarán na hÉireann. No excuse can exist that you officially or personally had no knowledge of the file on this occasion.

You make much of presenting yourself to us as Mr. Nice, the Man of the People, or as the media label you *the Presser of the flesh*. So, a Thaoisigh, let us start with the basics. Do you believe in innocence, childhood, kinship, family, probity, honesty, goodness, uprightness, truth, integrity, tenderness, honour, sincerity, fidelity, constancy, loyalty, fairness, justice, steadfastness, righteousness, consideration, compassion, sympathy, respect, attention, support, duty, responsibility, obligation, commitment, conscience, morality, ideals, standards, ethics, liability, accountability, virtue, belonging, promise, performance, security, fair dinkum, humanity, concern, care, regard, intimacy, Bunreacht na hÉireann/Constitution of Ireland, Forógra na Cásca 1916 Proclamation, The Universal Declaration of Human Rights, freedom, protection, citizenship, nationality, Irishness, faith, hope, love and life and all those genuine feelings of being a human being and an Irishman?

We do, a Thaoisigh. It is that belief in the goodness of people and much support of such goodness that has seen us through our horrible unspeakable years and months and weeks and days and hours and minutes of anguish and horror.

But the real question is: do you, Bertie Ahern? Even if your answer is yes, why don't you put your belief into practice rather than choosing to fail S., D. and us on all counts. Your choice, a Thaoisigh.

Taoiseach. What a glorious title. The most honourable title in EU politics, if not in the world. Now that you hold it for the third time by the grace of God and the will of the Irish people, what's your understanding of it, Bertie? Have you ever given it much or any thought? Have your multiplicity of highly-paid advisers ever discussed your very title with you or sought to define it in its depth and in its nature. One doesn't need a plethora of experts or a special Dáil Committee to do so. Look to Ó Dónaill: Foclóir Gaeilge-Béarla, page 1203, to understand such depth and such nature.

Taoiseach, 1. Hist: (a) Leader, chief; ruler. Taoiseach gach fine, the head of every family group (that qualifies us, too!). *Tiarnaí agus taoisigh, lords and chieftains. (b) First in order of rank. Taoiseach na mban, the foremost of the women* (which answers any question, which we do not share, of women's right to the position). *2. Pol: Prime Minister. 3. Man of substance; important person; decent, generous, person.*

When, Bertie, even in any one minute of our travails over the past 31 months have you been *decent* and *generous* to S., D. or us?

But Ó Donaill, the dictionary not the man, was not around when Bunreacht na hÉireann was being teased out and drafted and then enacted by the People on *1st July, 1937* and *in operation as from 29th December, 1937*. So we must look beyond Ó Dónaill to the lexicographical authority of the day, *Dinneen: Foclóir Gaedhilge agus Béarla, an Irish-English Dictionary* first printed in 1927 and reprinted with additions in 1934 in perfect timing for those charged with the preparation and writing of Bunreacht na hÉireann. Page 1173, *Taoiseach, a chief, head, leader or prince, a commander.* There follows a list of examples of usage from *taoiseach an bháis (Satan)* through *taoiseach loinge, a ship's captain* and *taoiseach fodhla, a master steward (one in charge of the division of meat, early)* to *taoiseach tána, a herd-leader, a ringleader, chief of a tribe.* No mention whatsoever of politics.

The nearest we envisage is chief in the Native American nations, responsible for life and death and judgement on one hand and on the other for providing for and guiding the well-being of his people and the protection and sustenance of the old and the young. We still await such protection whatever about sustenance from you, a Thaoisigh. To deny us such protection has been your choice to date. It is, however, a choice that Bunreacht na hÉireann does not allow you.

Within the subsection relating to the family of the Fundamental Rights section of Bunreacht na hÉireann (Constitution of Ireland) Article 41. 1. 1° and 2° are both specific and catholic: *The State recognises the Family as the natural primary and fundamental unit group of Society, and as a moral institution possessing inalienable and imprescriptible rights, antecedent and superior to all positive law. The*

State, therefore, guarantees to protect the family in its constitution and authority, as the necessary basis of social order and as indispensable to the welfare of the Nation and the State.

Our copy of the Concise Oxford Dictionary, which has served us well since 1974, page 436, defines family, 1. *Members of a household, parents, children, servants, etc; set of parents and children, or of relations, living together or not; person's children.* 2. *All descendants of common ancestor, house, lineage; race, group of peoples from common stock.* Of course, the word family takes us back through the centuries to Roman times and the word for household, *familias*. The Concise Oxford Dictionary was first published in 1911, with a new edition (revised) in 1929 and a third edition in 1934 again in good time for those charged with the drafting and preparation of Bunreacht na hÉireann (Constitution of Ireland) in both *the first official language, Irish,* and *a second official language, English.*

Such precision of delineation between **the first** and **a second** in Article 8.1 and Article 8.2 of Bunreacht na hÉireann is precedent, as anyone with a fluency in both official languages would know. Fortunately we are alumni of the De La Salle Brothers, na Bráithre Críostaí, the Franciscan Order and the Presentation nuns who instilled in us not only a lifelong gift and love of education but an equal facility in both Irish and English, a so valuable accomplishment not so readily achieved even by so many members of the Bar and of the Law Society. Indeed we were blessed to have been taught by two of the best teachers God ever put on this island, an Bráthar S. E. Ó Cearbhaill and an tAthair Odhrán Ó Duáin, O.F.M., to both of whom we are happy to acknowledge a lifelong debt of appreciation and gratitude. And so we can relate, as no doubt you can too, a Thaoisigh, those words of Article 8.1 and 8.2 to the all-embracing Article 25.5.4° *In case of conflict between the texts of any copy of this Constitution enrolled under this section the text in the national language shall prevail.* The final phrase in the same Article in the first official language is even more definitive *is ag an téacs Gaeilge a bheidh an forlámhas.*

Such definition, a Thaoisigh, takes us back to *an téacs Gaeilge* of

Article 41.1.1° and 2° which however specific and catholic it is in English as the Courts have upheld on numerous occasions, is even deeper and more direct in *an téacs Gaeilge:*

1. 1° *Admhaíonn an Stát gurb é an Teachlach is buíon-aonad príomha bunaidh don chomhdhaonnacht de réir nádúir, agus gur foras morálta é ag a bhfuil cearta doshannta dochloíte is ársa agus is airde ná aon reacht daonna.*

2° *Ós é an Teaghlach is fotha riachtanach don ord chomhdhaonnach agus ós éigeantach é do leas an Náisiúin agus an Stáit, ráthaíonn an Stát comhshuíomh agus údarás an Teaghlaigh a chaomhnú.*

As you have such a multitude of experts to advise you, a Thaoisigh, however tardy and neglectful they have been to date, we will focus on just two points, *Teaghlach* and *cearta doshannta dochloíte is ársa agus is aoirde ná aon reacht daonna.*

Teaghlach is a word cognitive of and expressing a definitive concept of Irish life back through the centuries. Again to *Dinneen: Foclóir Gaeidhilge agus Béarla,* page 1188, *Teaghlach, a family or household, familia or monastic family, an ethnic family or group, followers, escort; a house; t. Éanna, Éanna's familia; t. Táil, the Dalcassian stock. Teaghlach* not only underpins and gives full expression to the word *Family* in the English text but does it on the basis of usage of language on this island back to the dawn of history. It was not by accident but most deliberately that Dinneen dedicated his *Foclóir Gaeidhilge agus Béarla do Phádraig Mhac Calprainn Aspal agus Éarlamh Éireann* (to Patrick son of Calprann apostle and patron of Ireland). Such dedication was a statement by Dinneen that his dictionary ranged over the centuries drawing its sources at least from as far back as early 5th century Ireland and linking through St. Patrick to the Roman world and word, *familia.*

With full justification of lexicography, history and lineage, Teaghlach Uí L........ as founded by us on 30 August 1966, continues to the present day and as with many of the 1.053 million families of Ireland is rooted well into the dawn of Irish history. It behoves us and our 1.053 million compatriot families to safely guard what our Constitution recognises and look askance at anyone, political or otherwise, who would seek to pervert, alter or misappropriate any such rights of Teaghlaigh na hÉireann. Particularly, Bertie, a Taoiseach and a Government such as yours that has so utterly and so consistently failed to uphold the rights of our Teaghlach under Bunreacht na hÉireann over the past thirty one months. You did so by choice but a choice not yours to make under that same Bunreacht na hÉireann. You will be aware that in *an téacs Gaeilge* there is no *má, dá nó b'fhéidir* nor in the second official language any *if, might, but or perhaps*. Nor in either language is there any qualifying phrase, not even by reference to any other Article in Bunreacht na hÉireann. Article 41.1.2° is a stand alone precept of Bunreacht na hÉireann imposing a clear and unambiguous duty on the State:

The State, therefore, guarantees to protect the family in its constitution and authority.	Ráthaíonn an Stát comhshuíomh agus údarás an Teaghlaigh a chaomhnú

That includes us, along with all of the 1.053 million other families in this State. *Ráthaíonn/guarantees*, a Thaoisigh. Which of these two words do you and your whole administration and plethora of advisers not understand?

So, a Thaoisigh, why did you choose to ignore both us and Bunreacht na hÉireann? Why was there not one single person within your Government, tripping over itself with Ministers and Ministers of State that in numbers alone is a disgrace throughout the civilised world, to stand with our Teaghlach and Bunreacht na hÉireann? With such a small geographic area – not even the whole of one small island – and a total population of 4,239,848 people, in a world in which there are cities of three and more times our population – Shanghai, for example, venue for the 2007 Special Olympics has 20 million inhabitants – how could you so neglect any Irish family as you have Teaghlach Uí L........ and Bunreacht na hÉireann?

To illustrate the measure of your neglect we say to you that if S. and D. were hanging by their fingernails half-way down the

Cliffs of Moher you and all members of your extensive cabinet would be like Merriman's Hills of Clare, elbowing and jostling one another to get each face above the other for the photograph as you all tried to get aboard an Aer Corps helicopter for your political mercy trip.

Why across the whole range of highly paid Secretary Generals, top civil servants, experts and the armies of advisers has there been no one to say yes, the State has a duty to this Teaghlach, not just a duty of care but a duty of Constitution?

Abraham pleaded with God to save Sodom and Gomorrah for the sake of ten righteous men and we couldn't offer God even one righteous man to save the whole of your administration, centralised and decentralised. What a wasteland vision of your Ireland, a Thaoisigh, that such should be the case for any Irish teaghlach, that you should make a reality of those awful words of Joyce – or was it O'Casey? – *Ireland is a sow that eats its young?*

What standards and laws so blinkered and blinded you and your entire Cabinet to the ravaged innocence of three generations of an Irish family? What standards and laws so blinkered and blinded you and your entire Cabinet to the fate worse than death of an innocent three-and-a-half now six year old girl? What standards and laws so blinkered and blinded you and your entire Cabinet to the appalling fate of an innocent mother being forced by law to hand her only child over to the man who was abusing her from three years of age? What standards and laws so blinkered and blinded you and your entire Cabinet to the life at the Gates of Hell meted out, and supported by you, to an Irish family? What standards and laws so blinkered and blinded you and your entire Cabinet to the guarantees and protection and rights of our teaghlach under Bunreacht na hÉireann? Why with all that blinkering and blinding to good could you and your entire Cabinet embrace, support and be complicit in so much evil? How could we, a loving, caring, law-abiding and loyal family, in those circumstances be so shunned and shunted by you and your entire Cabinet? Does the stench of such sexual deviancy and paedophilia not reek in the nose of even one of all of you gathered around the Cabinet table, including yours, a Thaoisigh? How could your acceptance of and support for such perverse behaviour against an Irish citizen and an Irish family so cloud the judgement of your entire Cabinet and administration? You, a Thaoisigh, and all of you that have been so hypocritically vocal and vocally hypocritical of others both Church and secular during this very period of the past two and a half years. What did you and each member of your Cabinet do so differently in our case? You had full knowledge, all the horrible details. You took no action. You shirked your duty. You passed responsibility from pillar to post, from Billie to Jack, from Minister to Minister, never addressing the problem, never recognising our existence.

Few Provincials, if any, or lay chairpersons of organisations get a third term in office, but you did. No bishop, abbot, or sports activist has access to such resources as you, over €55 billion annual budget and armies of experts from law to psychology to education to human resources to medicine. Yet even with a third term in office and all these resources you still continue to choose to ignore us. Why? Even since you began your third term you have found time to spend days in that transient Temple of Mammon on a race course, welcoming and swanning and pressing the flesh with some of the State's greatest tax cheats, those who choose not to contribute to your salary, your perks or your pension, who don't even contribute to the public fuel bill for having you driven there and back. Yet you continue to ignore us as though we, one of this State's 1.053 million families, did not exist. Why, a Thaoisigh? And why did you go further against us? Why did you choose such evil over us and against us? Christ himself tells us *He who is not with me is against me* (Lk. 11.23). All the cold ashes of Lent cannot expiate that judgement.

Tell us, a Thaoisigh, where you and your entire Cabinet find authority in Bunreacht na hÉireann for your treatment of omission and commission against S. and D. and our Teaghlach over the past thirty-one months? Where in the whole of

Bunreacht na hÉireann, or indeed of The International Charter of Human Rights, did you and your entire Cabinet get authority for such woeful, scandalous, deleterious dereliction of duty and of care to this Irish family? You and your entire Cabinet have befouled yourselves in the waft and reek of such evil that serious questions must be asked not alone about our case but about others. We are not so naïve as to believe that our circumstances are so unique that we should be the only teaghlach out of 1.053 million to so suffer at the hands of you and your entire Cabinet. Which raises the fundamental question: as you and your Cabinet have rightfully pressed for the full audit and examination of others, who is going to undertake such audit and examination across the entire Cabinet and Departments of this State? We ask with Juvenal *quis custodiet ipsos custodes?*

2. *Cearta doshannta dochlóite is ársa agus is airde ná aon reacht daonna.* The emphatically simple words *ná aon reacht daonna* translate with such clarity and simplicity *than any human law* giving such universality and unquestionable definition *to all positive law.* How could any rational being have any difficulty in understanding the full and unfathomable import of such simple and all embracing words? No doubt, a Thaoisigh, your advisers will note too that Article 41.1° and 2° as a stand alone article is not dependant or related to any other article and furthermore in both official languages is so definitive that it excludes any doubt to its meaning.

Why then do you choose to stand over and effect the horrid shackles of an alien jurisdiction on behalf of a sexual predator? Do please explain to us and to the 1.053 million families in Ireland where in Article 41.1° and 2° you find your authority for such a choice. Why do you deny the rights and protection due each and every Irish teaghlach to us?

Such protection was, of course, offered to us but not delivered, by one of your Ministers, Mary Coughlan TD, Minister for Agriculture and Food in her letter to us of 5th May 2006 – S.'s fifth birthday: *I appreciate very much your anxiety and concerns about your family but the due process will have to be dealt with at Australian level, at which stage, once that court decision has been made, the Department of Foreign Affairs and the Irish State can institute, if necessary, protection arising out of the court decision.* That's pretty clear too, a Thaoisigh, even though to be true to Bunreacht na hÉireann it should read *will* rather than *can*. But under the horrific circumstances in which this promise was received we were not going to quibble. We do now because you, a Thaoisigh, have chosen to renege on both the *can* and the *will*. This promise helped to sustain us in those final horrific months in Sydney and together with the duress of being the only way open to us to get S. home to the safety of Ireland were our reasons to agreeing to such horrid conditions to achieve our objective and move back home from Sydney to Dublin.

We know of no greater duress than that a mother, D. should be legally forced to hand her child, S. over to a sexual predator who, having domestically abused D. for years had already begun to sexually abuse S. Yet on returning home we find that such duress doesn't count, is not recognised, can be set aside as though it never happened. Come off it, a Thaoisigh. Can you really be so callous? Can you really be so cruel? Can you really be so heartless? Never has a hostage come out of Iraq and be made to pay for anything done under duress. Even the British Ministry of Defence did not do so but flew their military naval personnel home, feted them on arrival, sent them home on leave and encouraged them to benefit financially out of their exploits if they so wished. Are you, a Thaoisigh, to continue to be infinitely more callous, more cruel, more heartless to an Irish family than the British Ministry of Defence has been to its personnel, trained in warfare and terror?

Whatever happened to Bunreacht na hÉireann under which we have lived all our lives? Whatever happened to the State in which we have lived all our lives? Whatever happened to democracy in this little State of ours?

About to become our longest serving Taoiseach and already one of the longest serving Presidents of the Republican Party, you like to protest your republicanism and admiration for Pádraig Mac Phiarais under whose portrait you sit at your desk. More than any other Irishman with the possible exception of Éamon de Valéra you have presided over more ceremonies at the nation's sacred ground, Arbour Hill. In all those visits have you ever listened to what those men of 1916 say? We have. Through 1961 we lived in the lodge of Arbour Hill where we enjoyed copious cups of tea with the incomparable Michael Biggs as he puffed his pipe with a relish known to few others so that smoke billowed from his mouth, his nostrils and even, it seemed, from every hair of his generous beard while his sparkling eyes and gentle voice conveyed the remarkable joy and kindness of the man. And we walked and sat among those holy graves through long summer days as Michael so meticulously cut the words of the seven signatories into stone in both official languages. And we listened to what those heroes had to say. For their words, like the words of the Gospels, are of and for the living – those who fought and didn't die – and that whole generation like your father and mother, a Thaoisigh, and ours, who lived and loved through those years of glory and shame that saw the dawning of the reality of the dream of those heroes become true, indeed, who made it come through and reared you and us to carry forward the development of that reality and to pass its fulfilment on to our sons and daughters and to our grandchildren, the S.'s of our youngest generation. And for S. and all of her generation that dream holds good. The words in stone on Arbour Hill and the heroes lying there still, as they always will, say: *The Republic guarantees religious and civil liberty, equal rights and equal opportunities to all its citizens, and declares its resolve to pursue the happiness and prosperity of the whole nation and all its parts, cherishing all the children of the nation equally.* Yet, a Thaoisigh, now in the fourth generation of those words, how have you dimmed the torch so much that horses are fed, watered, accommodated and doctored better, taxless or nearly so, than the 140,000 children in our capital city who go to bed, if they have a bed, hungry each night and S. and how many others are denied her/their basic rights and freedom envisaged in *cherishing all the children of the nation equally*. Amidst all the wealth of the last ten years how have you presided over a land of Houyhnhnms to the neglect of so many of our greatest blessings, our children. So much so that Irish children suffer greater deprivation than those in most wealthy countries. As the Unicef study earlier this year found, Ireland ranks 19th out of 21 industrialised countries for the proportion of children experiencing hardship.

What value do you and the Republican Party put on Poblacht na hÉireann as proclaimed at the GPO and sustained by Arbour Hill? We, like you, come of a generation who know that value. Through twenty years of summer holidays on the family homestead in Tipperary as must you on the farm of All Hallows College, we viewed and experienced and used that potent expression of Republicanism, the support of the dairy industry when it was far greater than it is now and in the days before milking parlours and quotas, that essential item of furniture in every cowhouse of the land, the three-legged stool. Liberté, Equalité, Fraternité. Saoirse, Comhionannas, Comhbhráithreachas. Freedom, Equality, Fraternity. And the greatest of these is Liberté / Freedom / Saoirse.

As you sit in Oifig an Taoisigh for your third term, what is your vision of the sacrifice that bought you that office? Do you ever look Pádraig Mac Phiarais in the eye and recall his vision of sacrifice for an Irish Republic:

Thugas m'aghaidh	*I set my face*
ar an ród seo romham	*on the road before me*
ar an ngníomh do tchím	*on the act I saw*
is ar an mbás do gheobhad.	*and the death I'd die.*

To us, a Thaoisigh, sacrifice is a small woman in black with bright eyes and long grey hair rolled in a chignon, quiet and dignified, so like that other distinguished lady, Sinéad de Valéra. Our lady lived on Mannix Road, just up the road from your own St. Luke's. She was seventy-eight when we moved in and eighty-two when we left. A quiet lady, reserved and discreet. It took some time before she told us her story. A young woman, mother of three children all under five, enjoying the freedom of a bank holiday on Easter Monday. She'd already fed and attended to the children and has begun to prepare the dinner, then the middle of the day meal. Husband, a grocer's assistant, resting on his day off as was his wont, a man of few to no words, came down the stairs and without speaking went out for a walk, again as was his wont. Did not return before dinner and when word and sound of revolution reached her, worries grew for husband and family, for without prior warning, she had neither extra milk nor food in. The neighbours were supportive. *Don't worry. Not him. Involved? Too quiet.* And as the shadows lengthened and the battle raged and darkness fell, *Aw he must have been across the bridge and couldn't get home. Don't worry, luv, he'll be home when things quieten down.* Through the week and through the worry there were three children to tend and feed. He didn't come home, with the ceasefire or afterwards. And there were still three children to care for amid constant worry and warnings not to *draw attention to yourself. Mind the Authorities.* Six horrifying weeks of waiting and worrying, traipsing with three young children around the hospitals and morgues of a ravaged Dublin. Until, finally, despite the Authorities, put her husband's photo in the Evening Mail. A Jesuit replied. *I buried that man in Glasnevin* and told the story. He was chaplain to the Children's Hospital in Harcourt Street, where there was an outbreak that week and children died but their bodies couldn't be moved because of the fighting on St. Stephen's Green and elsewhere. So as soon as the ceasefire was effected, the priest approached the British Army and was given a lorry to take the children's bodies to Glasnevin. As they passed the College of Surgeons, a soldier stood out in front of them and not knowing of the children said, *There's another one of them over there* and the body of a man was thrown in on top of the dead children and taken and buried in Glasnevin. On foot of this information that grieving and misfortunate woman then had to suffer the exhumation and identification of her husband's body. Despite all her travails, she went on with life, raising her three children, often scrubbing doorsteps to support them and herself and eventually losing the eldest as an RAF pilot over Gibralter. Seventy-eight when we arrived and eighty-two years of dignity when we left. She, a Thaoisigh, is sacrifice. Her name was Mrs Corcoran. Her husband, James. You'll find his name on the 1916 Roll of Honour. He was the first volunteer to die in the attack on the Shelbourne Hotel. That dear lady would have been doubly horrified at our circumstances today, firstly for all that we have and continue to suffer and secondly that the Government for which her husband, James, died and she so suffered, should act as you choose to. There is more to Republicanism than standing in front of cameras at Arbour Hill or the G.P.O. Along with the limelight, sacrifice and standards come wrapped in the flag.

There will be some, a Thaoisigh, who will tell you to ignore the Easter Proclamation and all that followed from it. This is modern Ireland and anyway the Constitution overtook all that. No doubt, a Thaoisigh, you'll be circumspect in relation to any such advice. As leader of Fianna Fáil you'll need to be for in the Easter Proclamation you'll find the only legitimacy for your full Party title – Fianna Fáil, the Republican Party. There is no mention of Poblacht or Republic in Bunreacht na hÉireann.

Like most of the 1.053 million families in Ireland (including the 1.053 million Taoisigh gach fine) we do have a natural and abiding interest in politics. Never card-carrying but sometimes close both practically and historically, including with your own party. Indeed we have enjoyed very happy experiences that have not been available to many of your current members. We have sat on public platforms with your founder, Éamon de Valéra, attended banquets at which he presided, had private meetings with him in Áras an Uachtaráin, played a part in the archiving and opening of his papers in the Franciscan House of Studies, Dún Mhuire, Killiney, including headhunting the inestimable An Dochtúir Breandán Mac Giolla Choille and his wife Éilis, to undertake that monumental task. We had a part also in the fulfilment of Éamon de Valéra's last will and testament that specified *Memorabilia* should be transferred to ownership of Ard-Mhúseam na hÉireann subject to their being put on permanent display in a President's Room, which we also helped bring into reality *pro tem*. We have even climbed those hallowed stairs in Áras Fhianna Fáil and gazed on that bleak portrait of the party's founder that doesn't do him justice and sat on an advisory committee to an advisory committee to you, a Thaoisigh, in that complex peripateticism that is Fianna Fáil. Not that any of these earned us any favours from you over the past two and a half years. Not, indeed, that we were looking for favours, just our Constitutional rights. No, we mention these as significant happenings in our lives and that we are proud of our part in them, so that lesser-minded party people will not accuse us of being anti-Fianna Fáil as we record happenings and neglects across a range of your Ministerial colleagues, all *ad rem*.

First to your own stewardship – a nice Gospel word, don't you think? – of An Roinn Gnóthaí Eachtracha, The Department of Foreign (formerly External) Affairs. For us it was always a Department with somewhat more attractiveness, even a touch of exoticism about it, as though imbued with a breath of Monsignor Pádraig de Brún's *Tháinig long ó Valparaiso* mystique. Forty plus years of such appreciation blown away by the reality of the past two and a half. Whatever attractiveness, exoticism and mystique there were stood on feet of clay. And when one is as deep in an abyss of misery as we were with those same feet pressing down on us, the only sight, if sight there is, is of those feet. And as an Roinn Gnóthaí Éachtracha had to figure (should have had to figure) prominently in our case we looked and looked.

A Thaoisigh, you've had four goes at appointing a Minister for Foreign Affairs. On your first, we rang one of your fellow travellers, cathaoirleach of a Dáil Ceantair, and asked one question: *What has Burke got on Bertie?* We could think of no other rational reason as to why you would have included him at any level in your Cabinet. We got no answer then nor since. But shortly you found yourself defending that same oh so honourable Minister in the Dáil right up to the bitter end claiming that such a man of honour was being *hounded out of office*. You replaced him with a safe pair of hands, David Andrews of old stock and one of our Teachtaí Dála in Dún Laoghaire for many years, still purposefully engaged with The Irish Red Cross. Next up was our current Aire Airgeadais, now Tánaiste, to whom we will return later. Finally, you handed the office and Department to your namesake, Dermot, whom you have recently re-appointed. In doing so you gave us a creation, a Thaoisigh, that outshines the genius of Swift, the wonder of Lewis Carroll and the combined fantasies of Hans Christian Andersen and the Brothers Grimm: a no-spotting, all-tree-climbing Minister for Foreign Affairs. If you'd only write a few chapters Aosdána might propose you for the Nobel Prize in Literature or the Arts Council nominate you for the Man Booker Prize for fiction. But for the moment we're left with the reality of your current choice in Iveagh House. All of what happened to us, what we suffered and at times almost seemed like we'd die for, happened on his watch. We believe he should, could and constitutionally was obliged to give us the support, the protection and indeed the relief we deserved. He didn't. He should have been advising you, prodding you if necessary. We can't say if he did, but we can say that you didn't give us the support, protection and relief we deserved either.

Dermot Ahern in this post was for us worse than a nonentity because we cannot conceive of anyone else in the office doing less. And so as former business consultants we do what we would have done in any professional personnel selection, look at the *c.v.*, look at achievements. Dermot Ahern has been in politics a long time, almost a lifetime and his greatest claim to fame is, in your own words, a Thaoisigh, *he climbed every tree in North County Dublin* and could find nothing on Mr. Burke. We know of no genus of monkeys that so wastes its time, so fruitlessly climbing trees. Nor, indeed, with respect to yourself, a Thaoisigh, was there any need to climb any tree. The dogs in the street knew what Mr. Burke had been up to for years, and not only the dogs of North County Dublin but our four-legged friends in Dún Laoghaire-Rathdown constituency too. A good question for future Fianna Fáil table quizzes would be *Which if any constituency didn't know?*

Mr. Ahern's next claim to fame is that as far as we've been able to ascertain he is the only man who was prepared, and did, take office in an island government with responsibility for Marine Affairs and agreed to take any reference to such responsibility out of his title. From fishing to transport, oil, gas, tourism, pleasure, coastal beauty/erosion, hygiene, bird life, climate change and drug-running, just to name some, how could any sane man ignore all and more of these elements on taking office – he, indeed, being from the fishing village of Blackrock in County Louth? Shortly after taking office as Minister for Foreign Affairs, he took himself at our (taxpayers, of course) expense to Washington, an area with which we respectfully suggest he was somewhat less familiar than North County Dublin. There, Condoleeza Rice had him for breakfast and without even waiting to recover and return to Ireland, Mr. Ahern in the most quisling of statements ever delivered by an Irish politician promised all but undying love to Miss Rice and the U.S. of A. in their troubles in Iraq. Within a few brief weeks of that meeting, Miss Rice's immediate predecessor, Colin Powell, and her Commander-in-Chief, George W. Bush, admitted that they both had misled the United Nations General Assembly in relation to Iraq. Mr. Ahern, to our knowledge, has yet to comment publicly on either of those admissions, while Miss Rice blithely continues to jet around the world like a neutered bee – all flight and no sting. Rosa Parks achieved infinitely more for all of mankind by sitting on a bus in Alabama.

On an equal level has been his monumental failure in relation to S., D. and Teaghlach Uí L........., which if allowed to stand will have the same serious consequences for others of the 1.053 million families in the State in the future.

You may not like our assessment, a Thaoisigh, but before you dismiss it, look to another Minister who held this position even under the former title, a Fianna Fáil Minister also from Co. Louth, and recall his stature at international level and how he bestrode the corridors and chambers of the United Nations like a colossus. He was, of course, Frank Aiken. It may have been another era, but it was a time when men were men and Government Ministers believed in responsibility and duty, both functionally and constitutionally.

We are old enough to remember honest Government in this State and young enough to care. While you bask in the glory of your third term as Taoiseach, you might remember that a little humility is good for the soul. Longevity of itself is no great feat, even in life, it's what we achieve with it. Look to Seán Lemass who hardly held office for half the time you have, and to the achievements of him and his Government and some brilliant public servants like Dr. Ken Whitaker in Finance and Dr. Tom Walsh in Agriculture. It was they, under Lemass's stewardship who set us, the Irish people, on the road to the economic success of the past decade over which it has been your privilege and good fortune to preside. Yet in all that success, that vast riches and wealth, you, a Thaoisigh, could neither find a moment nor a Euro for S., but chose to stand along with all of your Government with a man of evil. *If anyone gives even a cup of cold water to one of these little ones, I tell you the truth, he will certainly not lose his reward* (Mt 10.42). Not a cup of cold water from you to S. in over two and a half years of unbridled wealth, while in one instance alone you and your Cabinet could write off €190 million disastrously on only one failed project. Think of what a fraction of that money could have done for S. and other Irish citizens in trouble not of her or their own making. Now may be a different era but how can you and Fianna Fáil have fallen so low?

Christ himself has told us *By their fruits you will know them* (Mt. 7.20) and how well have we got to know them, each and every member of your Cabinet, the Minister of State for Children who also sits at the Cabinet table and Uachtarán na hÉireann. Yes, a Thaoisigh, we know Uachtarán na hÉireann is or should be above politics. Time was when we believed things to be so. We have lived and seen every Uachtarán from and including Seán T. Ó Ceallaigh in action. We have known or met four of these Uachtaráin and have been received both privately and formally at Áras an Uachtaráin. Indeed the only Uachtarán we have no living memory of is our revered first, Dubhghlás de hÍde. The selection process within Fianna Fáil from which the present incumbent emerged, shafted into office over the dead political body of your immediate predecessor in the best *Et tu, Brute* performance in Irish political and presidential reality has made her independence in office suspect from that moment on. That she should stand for office for the second term as an Independent does nothing to alter that reality, indeed, only copperfastens it.

*   *   *

So we turn to the first of those fruits by which we know you too well, the Minister for Foreign Affairs and his hugely funded and hugely staffed Department. It was to this Department that we first turned in January 2005 when things went from bad to worse and the tragedy and pain that was to unfold and engulf us was just beginning to emerge. Since then we have enjoyed the support of the Irish Consulate in Sydney and on a number of occasions in writing to you, a Aire, have acknowledged that support, including the accession to one of our early requests that the Irish Consul in Sydney would attend in support at Court. We have also acknowledged and are happy to do so again the enormous support of Anne Webster, the Consul General in Sydney during the first ten months of our ordeal. She is a lady of immense compassion and understanding, a lady of whom any country should be proud and a lady whom we were privileged to come to know.

From the outset we have kept the Department fully informed of every twist and turn in our evolving story, much of which need never have happened if the Department had accepted the completed application for S.'s Irish passport, which we had with us on that first day. Yes we knew it was out of date and yes we accepted far too readily your Department saying so. But eighteen months of the cruellest hostaging imaginable in conditions of constant fear, threat and terror, with our daughter D. forced by law to hand over her three, then four, then five year old daughter, S., twice each week to the man who began sexually molesting her at three and a half and as far as we know continues to do so as occasion allows, sharpens the focus and not only brings a new perspective, but forces it through and hones it. So why couldn't, shouldn't a validly completed passport application even if out of date be accepted in exceptional circumstances? Why hadn't the Department a process in place to do so? Could not the Department have a special committee to do so, within itself, within the Government, chaired by an tUachtarán, or even of twelve good men and women true? Does the Department yet have, or has it not learned lessons from our pain?

So what of our squeaky clean Department of Foreign Affairs? Could this be the Department (then External Affairs) which so covered itself in blood in 1945 that that blood still oozes through the carpet pile in Iveagh House? One of the United States' most sacred sites is not on continental America but thousands of miles out into the Pacific Ocean resting in about thirty feet of water in that place of infamous attack and heroic sacrifice known worldwide as Pearl Harbor. In that dawn attack on 6th December 1941, the U.S. Pacific navy was almost destroyed, with the U.S. Arizona taking its full crew with it as it sank in water less deep than its own riggings and superstructure. It remains the grave of those men, rendered now as a fitting, holy and evocative memorial to all who died in Pearl Harbor on that winter's morning, when the U.S. military and naval might still retained such honourable international standing. It is the United States basilica to heroism and to sacrifice. And still from the ship's tanks a globule of oil rises and gently surfaces about every minute or so, a poignant tiny movement in the stillness of sacred remembrance. No doubt, Minister, you've visited the shrine, as we have. Never to be forgotten. But there is nothing sacred about the blood in Iveagh House, oozing there since 1945 when your Department could put the requisite papers into Nazi hands dripping with the blood of a million people and permit that mass murderer, Andrija Artukovic, to escape from Switzerland into Ireland and be given safe haven in Rathgar, as the redoubtable Cathal O'Shannon recently reminded us on RTÉ television. Indeed, that blood will continue to ooze for far far longer, replenished with every military flight that lands at Shannon. Full facilities in 1945 for one of the great Nazi mass-murdering overlords of World War II and sixty years on not a dot on a line for an innocent mother and her three year old daughter.

Could this be the Department that hounded and decried an

octogenarian priest, the Jesuit An tAthair Diarmuid Ó Péicín, through New York, Washington and Capitol Hill itself for the crime of attempting to save the people of Tory Island from ejection by their own Government from their island home and the ending of that community? Yet so many years on and not a dot on a line for an innocent mother whose only crime is that of any Irish mother, that she loves her daughter more than herself.

Could this be the Department that so critically released certified confidential documents relating to Mary McAleese in a manner designed to damage her during her first Presidential campaign and by so doing, to pervert the democratic process of this State? How now for a simple private process for S. and D. and us?

Could this be the Department that watched with such dereliction of duty as the Brazilian Embassy just around the corner provided all necessary papers, transport and cash to spirit a convicted sex criminal out of this State and home to the bosom of his family in Brazil? Yet with both an Embassy and a Consulate in Australia you, Minister, and your whole Department, couldn't, didn't, chose not to, return two utterly innocent citizens, harrowingly being harassed, home to the bosom of their family in Dublin.

Could this be the Department that within the hour could admirably mobilise and activate all the resources and machinery at its disposal as well as at the disposal of the whole of the Government on receipt of the news of the hostaging of Rory Carroll in Baghdad? Within twelve hours his father confirmed that the whole family (and how deeply did we feel for them) was in *a state of deep despondency*. But no such action at all for S. and D. and this family, then fifteen months into our harrowing hostage situation.

Could this be the Department that invited to Ireland and feted the Honourable John Howard, prime minister of the country holding two innocent Irish citizens in hostage and terror for what was undoubtedly the most ignominious and disgraceful head-of-state visit in the history of this State? Could you, a Aire, ever have envisaged inviting Saddam Hussein who, for all his crimes did not force an Irish mother to hand over her daughter to the man who was abusing her, for a State visit? And Mr. Howard so ungraciously threw your hospitality back in your face and the faces of the Irish people with his brash berating of Irish Government policy in his address to Dáil Éireann and in his discourteous abrupt departure from Ireland ahead of schedule. For what Mr. Howard, his policies, his police, his legal and social systems did to this family, every Australian visa issued to any Irish citizen electronically or otherwise should be obliged to carry a heavy health warning from the Government of Ireland and all advertising and promotion to attract citizens from the whole of the European Union to emigrate to Australia should be immediately and permanently banned.

But, also, in fairness to Australia we watched in awe on television as its diplomatic representation in war-torn Lebanon, where we Irish have given such noble service, admirably coped with the repatriation of thousands and thousands – was it 20,000, Minister? – Australian citizens within two weeks in such dreadful conditions. While in contrast you and your Department with both Ambassadorial and Consular services in a non-war-zone country couldn't, didn't, chose not to, repatriate two innocent citizens, a mother and her three, then four, then five year old child over a full eighteen month period.

Could this be the Department with an expensive Embassy, Ambassador and staff in Canberra that never once acknowledged S. and D.'s existence through all of our nightmare. Not as much as a telephone call. Yes. Minister, we know you'll claim that we were in New South Wales and so came under the aegis of the Consulate in Sydney. But you know that's only part of the whole. Yes we were resident in Sydney, but the forces stacked against us and mistreating us were Federal, both the Federal police and State police, the Federal Court of Australia and the Family (sic) Court of Australia. We once visited our Embassy in Canberra, 20 Arkana Street, Yarralumia. We were on our way to pay our respects to our father's cousin, Monsignor J. B. Ryan, ordained in Thurles in 1919, who devoted his whole priestly life to the people of New South Wales, including some thirty-five years as parish priest of Cooma. He lived through the development and completion of the Snowy River Scheme, being an

EU Commissioner before ever the European Coal and Steel Community was founded, as he served a huge influx of migrant workers from central Europe (and from Ireland, of course), particularly Poles and Germans so immediate and bitter enemies in the aftermath of the Armageddon that was World War II. Our visit to the Embassy was unmemorable except for our disappointment to find a rather nondescript photograph featured in the waiting area. It was of a group of men including you, a Thaoisigh, standing on the steps of Sydney Opera House with your then partner slightly askew from the group with arms and legs akimbo like a caricature of a well over-seasoned ballerina. As we continued on our journey to Cooma we reflected on the gulf in standards with which Monsignor Ryan laboured and served the people of New South Wales as against this portrayal of standards at our Embassy in Canberra. C'est la vie!

As we the people of Ireland fund every aspect of this Embassy from pay-cheques, pensions and perks to telephone calls and stationery, please tell us, Minister, just what did the Ambassador and Embassy of Ireland in Canberra do for us over the eighteen months of our ordeal in Australia? Considering how the Ambassador and Embassy of Brazil in Harcourt Street, just around the corner from your office, could provide new papers including new passport for a convicted sex criminal to escape from Garda surveillance and be expatriated home to Brazil, surely the people of Ireland are entitled to know just what action was taken by our Ambassador and Embassy in Canberra on behalf of S. and D. and to an explanation as to how whatever efforts were made were so spectacularly less successful than those of the Ambassador and Embassy of Brazil in Dublin.

Could this be the Department that through its Irish Aid / Government Official Development Co-Operation Programme helped fund Amnesty International in Ireland to produce The Universal Declaration of Human Rights in very handsome form for framing and displaying and either didn't read it or, of it did, didn't heed it? No need to seek out the Department's copy, a Aire, or to read the succession of *Whereas*'s or all thirty Articles. Just Article 16(3) will suffice *The family is the natural group unit of society and is entitled to protection by society and the State.* Sounds familiar, Minister? Like a friendly echo of our own Article 41.1° and 2°, wouldn't you agree? Maybe even our Bunreacht na hÉireann enacted in 1937 was the model for The Universal Declaration of Human Rights which wasn't adopted by the General Assembly of the United Nations until 10 December 1948. And if ever you or your Department is tempted to invite Mr. Howard or one of his successors as Prime Minister of Australia for another disastrous visit, you or the Department should take the opportunity to direct his / her attention to Article 13(1) of the same Universal Declaration *Everyone has the right to freedom of movement and residence within the borders of each state.* And 13(2) *Everyone has the right to leave any country, including his own, and to return to his country.*

Could this be the Department that considers some 95% of parents and citizens of this State as unacceptable and untrustworthy to witness signatures on passport application forms? What plague of indiscretions so disqualifies the vast majority of parents and citizens of this State from such a simple and basic task? Why should your Department brand so many of us as dishonourable? Indeed, Minister, of your preferred categories of acceptable signatories, how many are so unblemished, so innocent, so upstanding, that they have not been touched by recent public scandals, including sexual abuse and/or paedophilia? Even more importantly, whatever happened to equality, to cherishing all the children of the nation equally? Whatever happened to Article 40.1 of Bunreacht na hÉireann:

1. All citizens shall, as human persons, be held equal before the law?.	*1. Áirítear gurb ionann ina bpearsain daonna na saoránaigh uile i láthair an dlí?*

Why, Minister, do you and your Department tell us both, with almost 130 years of honourable citizenship of this State between us, that we are not good enough to witness a signature to a passport application form, even in the harrowing circumstances in which it was required. Yet, you and your Department found acceptable the signature of a woman who was never closer to Ireland than 10,000 miles, who cannot spell either Éire or S., who wouldn't be able to find Ireland on a globe of the world, who was to be the long-threatened step-mother of S., who on one of her earliest meetings with S. told her that her mother didn't love her, who already has departed the scene and S.'s life forever, but who was and will remain forever more acceptable to you, Minister, and to your Department, than us and the vast majority of decent Irish parents, because she holds a chartered accountant's certificate close to her well-chartered breasts, indeed, knowing the people involved may well have signed the passport form during an *in flagrante* humping and thumping session – they are both well past the age of frolicking – as a grand gesture of respect to the Irish nation. That you, Minister Ahern, and your Department, should find such a signature acceptable over and above ours and that of some 95% of the parents and citizens of this State is an appalling indictment of all that you failed to do on S., D.'s and our behalf over the past two and a half years and a universal insult to the people of Ireland.

Could this be the Department that so prostituted itself that it sold the jewel in its keeping for nothing but money, no kith, no kin, no relationship, no connection, no history, no lineage, just money, enough of it and anyone could buy an Irish passport recognised and accepted around the world as the symbol and status of Irish citizenship? And its keeper, the Department of Foreign Affairs, sold it for nothing but money; and sold it so indiscriminately that one purchaser could produce a multiplicity of Irish passports in his defence against serious charges in the United States' Courts; and sold it so profligately that years later some billionaire purchasers could have their cake and eat it when they successfully applied to the High Court in Dublin earlier this year for the return of their purchase price while continuing to hold their Irish passports. What management in Grafton Street or on Fifth Avenue would so botch the sale of their store's pride and joy? Indeed, what local corner shop?

Could this be the Department that retains a huge global presence of Ambassadors around the world on behalf of, and at the expense of, us, the people of Ireland, yet can with that huge outlay, so crushingly fail any Irish family? Over the past two and a half years we have watched how Ambassadors can dirty their fingers from the Australian Ambassador in Baghdad up to his oxters in a Aus$400 million wheat scam to the U.S. multi-millionaire Ambassador in Dublin who (on behalf of the multi-billion dollar chewing gum industry) could buy off the Irish Government for a paltry €5/6 million, while you and your Department rated S., D. and Teaghlach Uí L…….. far less than chewing gum.

Finally, a Aire, could this be the Department and the Government that delivers far less to its citizens than what it requests on our behalf of other Governments? You have, no doubt, read the statement in both official languages inside the front cover of that most vital of booklets issued in your name and under the aegis of An tAontas Eorpach – European Union and entitled Éire Ireland Pas Passport. It reads:

Iarrann Aire Gnóthaí Eachtracha na hÉireann ar gach n-aon lena mbaineann ligean dá shealbhóir seo, saoránach d'Éirinn, gabháil ar aghaidh gan bhac gan chosc agus gach cúnamh agus caomhnú is gá a thabhairt don sealbhóir.

The Minister for Foreign Affairs of Ireland requests all whom it may concern to allow the bearer, a citizen of Ireland, to pass freely and without hindrance and to afford the bearer all necessary assistance and protection.

In both official languages it is a model of clear and lucid writing, utterly unambiguous in meaning and content – *gach cúnamh agus caomhnú is gá a thabhairt don sealbhóir / to afford the bearer all necessary assistance and protection.* Had we the opportunity to write it ourselves applicable to our own case we could not have done so any more accurately, concisely or truly: *gach cúnamh agus caomhnú is gá a thabhairt don sealbhóir / to afford the bearer all necessary assistance and protection.* Yet you, the Minister named, have consistently refused and chosen not to give that protection to S. How prescient of Christ to admonish us to listen to our lawmakers but not to do as they do, particularly those who would lord it over us, a child, a mother and one in 1.053 million families.

* * *

In December 2005 you stood in the limelight on the steps of Government Buildings with one wife, two daughters and a €56 billion budget brief-case. Television cameras whirled and news cameras flashed and made wonderful full-colour happy pictures for the following days newspapers. The Cowan family off on a €56 billion holiday. So impressive, so genuine that even we in all our anguish were, as they say in Éamon Ó Cuív's Connemara *meallta*, or in that so English word, *charmed*. So we wrote to you, Brian Cowan, strong upstanding family man and Minister for Finance, a special letter. Reminded you that you had all our story already and giving a special twist to it, relating it to your two daughters. Idyllic, almost, yet certain of a happy ending. But we had forgotten: we were writing to the man of no heart, to the man who given the privilege and responsibility and being well-paid and generously privileged to do so, had described the care and welfare of the most needy of our people, the sick, the diseased, the dying, the pained, the suffering, the elder citizens who had kept this shaky economy of ours afloat during times of need and had kept faith with Fianna Fáil through much of their lives, as *Angola*. None of that stuff about *I was sick and you looked after me* (Mt 25.36) or *Whatever you did for one of the least of these brothers and sisters of mine, you did for me* (Mt 25.40). That kind of stuff is all right if you're looking for votes in Tullamore but in the nerve centre of Government Buildings stronger even than the Temple in Jerusalem we can do fine without that kind of humanity not to mention spirituality. God made my term here the richest in the history of the State and by God, He better stay out of it until I'm finished. I'm Brian Cowan and I'm going to the top. Bertie says so.

Compassion doesn't cost anything, is never a burden on a private or the public purse. Most of us have it to give and those who don't often end up needing it most. Remember the advice of the poet *Go réidh a bhean na dtrí mbó*. Or refresh yourself on St. Luke's – gospel, Brian, not Drumcondra headquarters – the parable of the sick fool who had *plenty of good things laid up for many years* (Lk.12.19). Or indeed think of two former Fianna Fáil holders of high office, Charlie McCreevy who thought he was at the height of achievement and expectation and had the rug pulled out from under him with the Groom's Hotel offer of *"a pint or a transfer, sergeant"* only there was no pint on offer from you-know-who; and Albert Reynolds who was actually shown the ballot paper but not the knife by you-know-who too. We weren't *meallta* or *charmed* so much as conned, which we realised as soon as we received your reply: *get yourselves a legal team in Sydney*. This from, we would have thought, the best Minister around the Cabinet table being a solicitor to understand the hardships and disappointments we had suffered in trying to do just that, with no resources. And this from the best person around the table to have a realisation of the costs involved.

Do tell us, Brian, how many families in the environs of Tullamore can come up with Aus$141,000 and €5,600 unexpectedly and urgently late in life? Do tell us, Brian, how many families in the environs of Tullamore in which the principal earner had been struck down with illness for close on twenty years and had lost the capacity to earn and had to draw on all reserves to survive can then come up with Aus$141,000 and €5,600 unexpectedly and urgently late in life? Do tell us, Brian, how many families in the environs of Tullamore in which the principal earner had been struck down with illness for close on twenty years and had lost the capacity to earn and had to draw on all reserves to survive and had at no time become a burden on the State can come up with Aus$141,000 and €5,600 unexpectedly and urgently late in life? These were just the legal bills, no travel, no living expenses included. But then we remembered one latent asset, so long on the back-burner that we had almost forgotten. £50,000 – a somewhat familiar figure now in St. Luke's and elsewhere – that Charlie McCreevy had decreed should be held in trust until we reached seventy-five. So we wrote to you and to An Taoiseach to authorise the release of this money for S.'s defence. We also wrote to David Went, head of Irish Life, delivering all three letters by hand on the same morning – those to An Taoiseach and yourself shortly after 8.00 a.m. and David Went's at Irish Life's reception desk at 8.40 a.m.

By the time we reached home precisely two hours later travelling by public transport, there was already on our answer-phone a reply from Irish Life, with contact name and direct telephone number of the person most relevant to help us. We sat down and cried at the wonder of such an efficient and positive response from a commercial company in contrast to no response to action across the full range of Government Departments in Dublin over a period of almost fifteen months. In all the constant and intense darkness of that fifteen months and since, that telephone call was not just a shaft but a beacon of light and hope that still shines in our lives today.

But, however promising and despite Irish Life's best efforts, even this effort brought no success. For though you and An Taoiseach wrote to inform us in An Taoiseach's own words *The matter of the encashment of this policy is between you and the company* the ogre of the Revenue Commissioners, Na Comisinéirí Ioncaim, raised its insensitive and unfeeling head. No £50,000 for S.'s defence fund. One must ask how a State that had recently allowed an **overrun** of €8-12 billion depending on who was calculating to one arm of the public service could feel so financially threatened by petty cash considerations (though huge to us) of £50,000.

Who are these Revenue Commissioners, so much more powerful than Irish Life, the Minister for Finance and An Taoiseach? Could they be the same people who had so consistently failed the people of Ireland through the Sixties, the Seventies, the Eighties and even into the Nineties, believing as did Leona Hemsley, recently deceased, that *Only little people pay taxes*? Could they be the same people who nonchalantly strolled across the courtyard of Dublin Castle to tell the Tribunal that yes we were afraid of Charles J. Haughey? Could they be the same people that now that they have woken up to the realisation that more than little people should pay tax still admit that they know that they should be getting more in settlements (when did that leniency apply to our 1.053 million families mostly in the PAYE sector)? Could they be the same people who within their own rules facilitate if not conspire with the very wealthiest in our society to ensure that they pay minimal, even no, tax at all? Could they be the same people who had almost broken our hearts and cost us a lot of money from 1974 on – and continue to do so – so that eventually their own Cathaoirleach/Chairman had agreed that we should meet to put things right – and that was fifteen years ago and we still await the meeting? Could they be the same people who could give Ben Dunne an instant hearing, but then we didn't have Charles J. intervening for us? Could they even be the same people who recently wrote to tell us they owe us money? Could it be . . . could it be . . . almost beginning to sound like the song out of Joseph and his Amazing Technicolour Dreamcoat. Not a bad anthem for a Minister for Finance. Joseph after all was the guy who knew what to do with seven good years.

Then it was St. Patrick's Season - Day for the little people who pay taxes, but Season for those who spend them. You drew Sydney. The Irish people transported you there in comfort befitting your position, set you and your retinue up in equally befitting accommodation and generally treated you in a style becoming of a Minister of any rich country, picking up the tab for all. Yet at the Consular reception, again paid for by the Irish people, there was a young lady, D., who could have done with a word of cheer maybe even of hope, along with her daughter, S., hard to miss in any room with her lovely long red hair. But you did, miss her we mean, Minister. A man with a €56 billion budget supplied by the Irish people and not a word, not a smile to give to a young Irish citizen horribly entrapped twelve thousand miles from home.

How monstrous, Minister. Even Frankenstein in that touching scene when he meets the young girl evokes feelings and emotions almost human, but not you, Minister. The man with neither compassion in his heart nor music in his soul will always be a poor man among the rich of the world. For complicity in all S., D. and we have suffered you should have long since underwritten all of our expenses. You didn't, but family and good friends and the best Credit Union in the world, Glenageary/Sallynoggin, did. You should have long since taken on board an early recommendation that we made to Government that a special fund to help Irish citizens abroad with special and urgent needs be set up and you didn't. What difference would €5 million or, indeed, €25 million make to a €60 billion budget, particularly when it needn't come out of proper expenditure but out of the Waste Fund? You've just, as Minister for Finance, seen without demur, another €190 million washed down the drain by the Health Service Executive then left your office and gone home to dinner.

Michael McGuirke has not gone home to dinner. He languishes as we write, in intensive care in La Ribera Hospital in Alzira, Spain, after an accident. €20,000 will bring him home for treatment and to the comfort of his family. What's €20,000 to your current Waste Fund? But oh, the difference to Michael and the McGuirke family.

Your colleague in Foreign Affairs has laudably set up a unit for Irish victims of tsunamis but even the most basic of surveys would show that we as a people are far more likely to fall foul of a plethora of other accidents and misadventures, equally painful, equally fatal, less dramatic maybe but nonetheless real for that.

With such lack of compassion, even silence, towards our case you'll understand, Minister, our amazement at how vociferous you could be and are in support of Bertie's £50,000. Not even a matter of either ethics or morals. Absolutely correct and above board. Legitimate. If it was, why hasn't he done so regularly since? £50,000 even into a Minister for Finance's or Taoiseach's back pocket is not to be sniffed at. Or does it mean that you yourself have or will be collecting the occasional dig-out in Manchester or elsewhere. For now that the principle has been set, why not? And will it always remain the prerogative of the Minister for Finance or can anyone around the Cabinet table cash in? For someone who couldn't even say *Hello* or *Dia dhuit* to S. and D. you certainly found your voice on behalf of Bertie. Your voice, but your words? There must be a good Ph.D. thesis in an analysis of the debate surrounding the political demise of Ray Burke and the political survival of Bertie Aherne. Same hymn sheet with a slight tweaking of the lyrics here and there. And a bulling voice to deliver, so that those wise words of a wise man, aired on our national airways, resonate as a chorus: *A fool always finds a greater fool to admire him.* No doubt you fully concur with that wise man for that wise man was none other than Brian Cowan, Minister for Finance.

And are we to believe that Miriam was so passionately ruthless or so ruthlessly passionate as to so destabilise the second most powerful politician in the country who throughout enjoyed the support of the Government of this State that he was unable to maintain a bank account? Are we to believe that Miriam was such a harridan? Are we to believe that this harridan is mother of his two beautiful daughters? Are we to believe that this is the reality of the cosy relationship that is now presented to the people of Ireland with Miriam along to support him for the recent election? Are we to believe this of the gentle lovely lady we see smiling out at us from our newspapers? We think not. Do you, Minister?

Tell us, a Aire, how could we have survived all our trauma without the support but rather the complicity of the Irish Government throughout. And tell us, Minister, if we for all our trauma and lack of resources can maintain a long-term savings account in the Bank of Ireland in O'Connell Street, just a few steps from the now famous / infamous branch of A.I.B., with only a princely balance of €1.19 then for one Minister of Finance – former and now Taoiseach – supported by another Minister for Finance – current and also Tánaiste with pretensions to be Taoiseach – to trumpet the lack of a bank account as a basis and excuse for much of the dreadful, unholy and unhealthy financial curmudgery of Bertie Ahern shows that the rottenness in this State at the highest level smells to the core of Government. Can the level at Cabinet where we looked for support and protection for our family be so base?

At no time in all you had to say in defence of An Taoiseach did you avert to the half-million Euro he as leader of Fianna Fáil receives yearly from the public purse. Or the four and a half million Euro paid from the same source annually into the coffers of Fianna Fáil. Please don't insult the intelligence of the Irish people by telling us that Fianna Fáil has systems in place. Nothing happens in Fianna Fáil without the knowledge and sanction of Bertie Ahern. From the largesse of Ben

Dunne, the stealth of Michael Walls, the sleaze of dig-outs, the tsunami of brown envelopes, the sacrilege of the Temple of Mammon and the unnerving demands on the public purse, is there no end to the rapacity and voracity of Fianna Fáil for other people's money?

As with money, so with behaviour: from the crimes of Ray Burke to the illegalities of Beverley Flynn and Michael Collins and the Tribunal catalogue of cash for votes. Yet for our grand-daughter, our daughter and our family not a Euro, not a word. When did the man you so vehemently support in pocketing dig-outs last stand on a forecourt, fill the tank and do as every other mother and father have to do, put their hand in their pocket and pay? When last did he stand in the sun or the rain at the bus-stop next to St. Luke's and take a bus into the city centre like so many of the taxpayers of this country? For all of his public enthusiasm for the Dubs when did he last pay his way into Páirc an Chrócaigh? Thousands and thousands of Irish families would rejoice in such privilege even to stand on The Hill or to sit at the Canal end, just once. Indeed, Minister, when did you?

How many Fianna Fáil members of Government arrive at the Temple of Mammon, for the sole purpose of feeding Fianna Fáil's rapacity and voracity for money, in the top of the range transport funded by Irish taxpayers for their Government duties? And then sit down with some of the biggest cheats of the Irish people and of your own Department.

Has the age of Fianna Fáil blank cheques passed from Upper Mount Street to Upper Merrion Street to be extended an universal seal of approval by the Minister for Finance? Is the Minister for Finance a shadow Keeper of the Party's Purse or can he be other than a sinecure Keeper of the Public Purse, paid, perked and pensioned by the Irish taxpayers?

Over all the talk is the important issue of the spiralling cost to the public. Irish taxpayers pay for Ministers to attend to matters of State not of Fianna Fáil. Don't you think, Minister, that someone like the Comptroller and Auditor General should do a cost analysis on the time and facilities of Government devoted to digging out Bertie and send the bill to Fianna Fáil?

From the departure of Ray Burke to the imminent second coming of Beverley Flynn, nothing so sums up the history of Fianna Fáil under the man you so vociferously defend as those two classic lines – slightly adapted – of Alfred Lord Tennyson:

Its honour rooted in dishonour stood
And faith unfaithful kept it falsely true.

Thank God we have Bunreacht na hÉireann. Its writ holds even in the Department of Finance. It will yet vindicate S.'s, D.'s and our rights, *do chum glóire Dé agus onóra na hÉireann* as the old masthead on The Irish Press used daily proclaim. Just check the opening sentence of Article 40.1 of Bunreacht na hÉireann under Fundamental Rights / Bunchearta, Personal Rights / Cearta Pearsanta: -

All citizens shall, as human persons, be held equal before the law.	*Áirítear gurb ionann ina bpearsain daonna na saoránaigh uile i láthair an dlí.*

– and explain to the 4,239,846 other citizens of this State where you, our Tánaiste and Minister for Finance, get your authority to devote such resources of time and finance of this State to Bertie Ahern's defence when you have consistently chosen to do the very opposite in our case. Please also explain to the 1.053 million families of this State why the affairs of one family even in travail should have such interminable call on our national resources and agencies, while another in travail for over two and a half years received nothing but a jackboot so big it requires a Fianna Fáil and Progressive Democrat hybrid foot to fill.

Yet we hope. *Hope springs eternal*. We hope and pray. Perhaps the road from Tullamore will be your road to Damascus. A big ask, we know, but the God of the Irish, now far less acknowledged in the corridors of power, worked such a transformation on Saul of Tarsus. Why not on Brian of Tullamore? Then perhaps even you, a Aire, will have a word of recognition, of comfort, of hope, and maybe even more than words for S., D. and us before next you stand on the steps of Government Buildings with one wife, two daughters and a budget brief-case of as yet to be determined how many billion Euro.

* * *

Mary, we believe in being straight. It's in us by nature. One of the first and still real maxims for us in life is *Fool me once shame on you. Fool me twice shame on me.* Like so, so many of our 1.053 million other married couples we had by Government decree to forfeit one of our careers on our wedding forty-one years ago today, 30th August 1966. Following Brian Goggin's subsequent rise from the bottom branch to the top of the tree in Bank of Ireland, thus may have ended by Government decree a career however nascent that might have ended in similar fashion with the first ever female Group Chief Executive in such an exclusive male bastion. You came later to love and marriage, let's say delicately somewhat after the bloom of youth. All the more should your choice of husband have given you pause as Tánaiste and senior Minister in a cash rich, expansionist and economy driven Government and cause to review your position. That you did not see, or chose not to see, the obvious conflict of interest between your love and your work in marrying into IBEC the greatest lobbying organisation in the State is indeed worrying. That not one of your Cabinet colleagues did not see, or chose not to, is beyond negligence. That An Taoiseach, when your resignation was not forthcoming, did not seek it was seriously derelict in his duty. And that he should reappoint you to the same post following the last election and that you should accept shows the moral high ground on which you purport to stand is in fact a quagmire. Yes, we know, Mary, you will claim that your husband is now retired. We are not aware of any senior IBEC, or indeed of its constituent forebears the FUE and CII, man (they are inevitably men) changing his spots between retirement and the hereafter.

As Tánaiste and Minister for Health and Children you had three great reasons, responsibilities and duties along with huge standing to ensure that the case of S. and D. and Teaghlach Ui L........ should have received the protection due to us of this State. Tánaiste is next to Taoiseach in its profound meaning, its history, lexicography and usage. That this was recognised by those who prepared Bunreacht na hÉireann is evidenced by the fact that it is the only word, other than Oireachtas, in both texts with no English equivalent. Tánaiste is Tánaiste in both official languages.

So, as Tánaiste for much of the period of our horror and terror in Australia you held an exceptional position of influence and power on all our behalves. You chose not to use it. In so doing you left a young mother and her child to languish as hostages to a sexual predator and molester of S. and to a system inimical and cruel to those two innocent Irish citizens. It must rank as one of the most churlish and cruel decisions of any Tánaiste in the history of this State, matched only perhaps by that of your immediate successor, Michael McDowell, to do likewise. In all three roles, as Tánaiste, Minister for Health and Minister for Children, you were fully aware of every gruesome and unhappy detail. Yet in all three roles you chose not to act.

We even asked at one point what Government, what legal system, what social system would insist on putting a four-year-old child in an infecting environment, MRSA or any known or unknown infection. As Minister for Health and Children, you didn't even reply. How could it be that you, with such relevant titles, with a specific Minister of State for Children sitting at the Cabinet table with you, with one of the greatest budgets among huge departmental budgets, and with an army of highly-qualified and highly-paid experts and specialists across the whole range of medical, psychological and social fields, that you, a Thánaiste, could not find a delegate, even one person, a) to contact us and b) to contact us with positive purpose? Is there not one active and positive person across the whole range of both of your Departments now that you are back in charge of them again?

Paedophilia, what a misnomer, in its Greek original means love of children. Change love to lust. The sole aim of the paedophile is to sexually abuse children. Any intimations of concern, care, friendship or affection towards the victim are always only a means to an end. That end is sexual abuse, preferably child sexual assault, because every case of abuse is a case of assault. It's not a new curse. Even in relatively modern history Freud was writing about it in 1896 including the results from abuse by an adult *all too often, a close relative*. We now know, of course, here in Ireland, as elsewhere, the paedophile can be anyone, father, brother, uncle, priest, judge, politician, social worker, doctor, teacher, Government adviser, sports coach or any other category you wish to name, Minister. Few generalisations can be made except that most paedophiles are male. Female paedophiles do exist but rarely and even then may be dominated by a male partner who is the primary offender. The price of security is constant vigilance. Almost impossible. Take away the almost when one's Government is complicit in the abuse, backing the abuser and insisting that he should have not only his way but also his opportunity.

Last March before D. had to take S. to Sydney, we, parents / grandparents, (D. is prohibited by Court Order, unbelievable but true) approached the HSE again for protection. No protection. So, Minister, let us tell you what happened to a five year old child. Taken from her bed and home at 4.00 in the morning, driven to Dublin Airport, cried all the way to Frankfurt, continued on to Singapore and Sydney, 30 hours in all, exit arrivals and her mother and constant loving companion and sole (along with ourselves) caring support had to hand her daughter over to the man who has been molesting her since she was three and he, unsupervised, took her for three weeks, returning her to her mother at the same airport. Do please, Minister, find us one expert in either of your Departments to convince us that that was in the best interest of S. Do try so yourself, Minister.

S. has told us little about that three weeks but she has told us that they spent part of the time in Queensland in some kind of a mobile home and that they both slept in the same bed. Do please, Minister, find us one expert in either of your Departments to convince us that that was in the best interest of S. Do try so yourself, Minister.

Roberge (1976) defined child sexual abuse as the *involvement of dependent, developmentally immature children and adolescents in sexual activity that they do not fully comprehend, are unable to give informed consent to, and that violate the social taboos of family roles*. Child sexual abuse occurs when an adult uses his or her power to force, entice or persuade a child to take part in sexual activities. A child is never in a position to make a choice about inappropriate sexual acts. Nor is there any way a child can depict explicitly the details of sexual acts performed on him or her unless the child has experienced them; his or her life does not typically involve exposure to such happenings. Sexually abused children have been known to deny, minimize, confuse, even claim to "forget". Research by Lucy Berliner and colleagues in Seattle has matched children's statements and later admissions by sexual offenders and found that not only were the children's statements accurate, but often were found to be understated accounts of the abuse suffered.

Why do you in this your second coming as Minister for Health and Minister for Children refuse, deny, ignore S.'s clear, unequivocal and frightening revelations? Perhaps you might listen to Dr. Kevin Browne, Director of the post-graduate programme in Criminological Psychology at the University of Birmingham, who has conducted a series of workshops on prevention and treatment of family violence, physical and sexual child maltreatment, at the Psychology Department of University College Dublin: Close blood relatives *coerce the child into sexual abuse through a long process of grooming. They portray to the child that sexual abuse is an education or game that won't do them any harm. They often share a home* (make that bed as in S.'s case) *with the child . . . I would say that there is a very big difference between a sexual abuser and a physical abuser in one particular aspect, in that* **sexual abuse can never, ever be accidental** (our emphasis). *Sexual abuse of a child is planned, especially in the home environment, over a long period of time. The offender begins to exclude the female adult partner and to come between the mother and the child. He turns the child into a sort of "Daddy's girl" or "Daddy's boy". This occurs through long and careful planning. It is an intentional act whereas physical abuse is often impetuous . . . We can't ever cure them.*

If necessary, also, Minister, get one of your experts to explain why a child being abused tells so little. There are many reasons, among them that S. has been telling her Mammy, the constant love source in her life, of this abuse for half of her young life and nothing has changed. So why should she continue to talk about things she doesn't like? She may even have begun to accept them as a normal part of her life and/or feel that Mammy doesn't care anyway. S. doesn't know the pain and anguish we've all felt and still do, nor of the unbelievably superhuman efforts we have made to keep her safe, nor does she know that two Governments and all their agents are stacked up against those efforts.

And that, Minister, is only now. Among the long-term prognosis are high morbidity in physical and psychiatric disorders and likely high premature mortality due to alcohol and drug abuse, chronic physical even sexual diseases and suicide. By then, of course, Minister, you (and we most likely) will be gone, and while it may not be a worry to you then it is to us now, who will be there for S? Our Courts almost daily record such horrors.

On your watch, Minister, S., as one expert recently put it has only to cope with: *The harm caused by child sexual abuse is immeasurable. For a large number of victims, there are the consequences of brutal and forced sexual penetration including bruising, tears to the perineal area, venereal disease and other infections and urinary tract problems. Immediate psychiatric concerns include a wide variety of behavioural and emotional problems, such as sleep disturbance, nightmares, compulsive masturbation, precocious sex play, disturbed relationships with peer groups and parents and regression of behaviour such as loss of toilet training skills.* No wonder the Good Book says *Sufficient for the day is the evil thereof* (Mt. 6.34). While we continue to be there for *the evil thereof*, where are you, Minister, and your experts of two Departments? Have we got to wait in horror until you hear the screams from Sydney or have the child's blood flow on the Cabinet table as we told you a year ago? Will you act now, Minister, before S.'s next trip at Christmas or will you just turn up like some Marie Antoinette amid the Snowmen to wave her off? What of the message in your recent *Parents Who Listen, Protect* booklet? We love the line: *Protecting children is everybody's business.* We've been singing it to you and your Cabinet colleagues for over two and a half years. Perhaps you should get out a special edition, **Ministers Who Listen, Protect**. Just as it says in Bunreacht na hÉireann.

* * *

We have travelled the roads of the two Ridings of Tipperary too, Minister. From Carrick-on-Suir, Clonmel, Cahir, Tipperary, Emly and on to Effin in Limerick. From Ballyneale to Ballina, from Skeheenarince to Redwood Bog. We've stood on Derrynaflan and in the valley of Sliabh na mBan. We've climbed Galteemore and tasted the icy purity of the water at its summit. We've stood by Christ the King and viewed the depth and breadth and beauty of the Glen of Aherlow. We've been to Bansha and paid our respects to Canon Hayes and to our kinsman poet, Darby Ryan, who sang the beauties of the Glen and of Ireland in so many pastoral lines in both Irish and English yet is mostly remembered for his ballad *The Peeler and the Goat*. We've looked on Charles Kickham so steadfast in Tipperary town and we've rambled through his Knocknagow in book and in Drangan and Mullinahown. We attended by invitation the re-dedication of Holy Cross Abbey with our dear friend An Dochtúir Tomás Ó Muiris officiating and An Cairdinéal Tomás Ó Fiaich, another great friend, presiding. On quieter days we've been on the roof of the Abbey's tower looking out over the vale between the Devil's Bit and the Rock of Cashel, both interminably linked in story and mythology. We've walked the Stations of the Cross and the peaceful Prayer Garden, monuments, along with her promotion of Padre Pio, to your dear mother's work, work indeed that will still be yielding a hundred-fold when Celtic Tigers and even Fianna Fáil will have faded into memory. We have sat, and served somewhat, with your father on one of his many projects in the Seventies when the principals crossed both sides of the political divide to include George Russell of Limerick and Fine Gael on the board of Michael Whelan's great dream of oil, Aran Energy. We have gamboled and played along the Comea Road, saving hay in the nostalgic summer days, delivering milk to Grantstown Creamery, long since redundant, and trotting and cycling past the Mansergh estate on our many trips to Tipperary town. We have drawn our first breath in Cashel, worshipped in St. John The Baptist Church and sat in class next door with the Presentation Sisters. We have walked Liberty Square on quiet nights and even quieter early mornings. We have known the glory and the pain of Munster Final days. We're conversant with the unhappy links of the Ursaline Convent to the musical career and infamous adventures of William Wallace. We sat and wined and dined and slept in Hayes Hotel, the birthplace of the G.A.A. We recall with relish our first visit to Croke Park, entrance through the schoolboys' because girls weren't expected gate for sixpence, on that first Sunday in September 1951 when Tipperary stymied Wexford's efforts to take the Liam McCarthy Cup for the first time. In later years we were proud and pleased to play some part, however small, in the transformation of the Sports Field into Semple Stadium. We even persuaded Sam Melbourne to bring some of his wonderful collection of G.A.A. *memorabilia* to Hayes Hotel and planted the seed in his mind that eventually saw him hand over his historic collection to the care of Croke Park. Ardfinnan, Clonpet, Rearcross, Ballycahill, Roscrea, you name it, Mary, and we've been there. Back through the dawn of history or as Yeats has so beautifully put it *Beyond the mists of twice ten thousand years*, long before ever there were county delineations and attachments we were there. Our filial bones lie in every parish in the county before ever there were parishes. Our bones lie with kings and archbishops and harpists on Cashel's St. Patrick's Rock and with Seán Tracey on the hill of Kilfeacle, just across the road from St. Patrick's Church. We have followed Patrick Sarsfield's ride from Killaloe to Ballyneety, walked with Dan Breen along the road to Solohead Beg and across the county border to Knocklong and stood by Father Theobald Matthew on the road to Golden. Like you, Mary, we took the road to Dublin but long before you. We came to settle, to raise our family and contribute to our community in Cabinteely and Dún Laoghaire. Years later you followed but in pursuit of your career, first nobly as a teacher and then into politics.

So when we were in our deepest abyss, when neither the legal system nor the tea and sympathy of Foreign Affairs were going to alleviate our horror, and we realised that we had to go the political route we turned to you, Mary Hanafin. There were so many reasons to do so, not least being that you were one of our Teachtaí Dála, you were a Government Minister, you had been Minister of State for Children, you shared with us a fluency in both official languages and you were a woman. Of course that was in the days when we believed all women, even politicians, had a heart.

We wrote to you from Sydney giving you brief details and requesting to meet you on our return some weeks later. We received no reply. Like Pearse's Bean tSléibhe

Do ghlaoigh mé ort
is do ghlór níor chuala,
Do ghlaoigh mé arís
is freagra ní bhfuaras.

Finally we did get through to the first and only S.S. officer we've ever come across anywhere in the world. He gloried in the title of constituency director or manager or something with an arrogance intended to brush all but his point of view aside. The fate of a young child, a then four year old child, and of our family was of much more importance than overbearing arrogance from any source, but even when we eventually reminded him that we thought we still lived in a democracy he still held the view that the Minister could do nothing for us in relation to matters in another jurisdiction while we pained in Dún Laoghaire, and offered to put it in writing. An offer we accepted. Two hours later he rang back. The S.S. officer had now reformed, or been leashed, and told us that the Minister would meet us. Which you did, and after recognition and polite words, you seemed to take interest as you took notes. Whatever about the notes, the interest at best was transient. You never delivered a thing – neither compassion even nor hope. As our Teachta Dála you should have delivered that much and more. But you chose not to. You could, and should, have brought our case to An Taoiseach and/or to Cabinet. You chose not to. You could, and should, have brought us encouragement. You chose not to. You could, and should, have done all of these things because you, like us, have the facility to read Bunreacht na hÉireann in both official languages with the same ease. Few other Ministers, nor An Taoiseach, can. We can only think of two others, Micheál Ó Máirtín and Éamon Ó Cuív. But you chose not to. The fate of a four-year-old girl now six and of her family in Dún Laoghaire meant nothing to you. Such heartlessness from a girl we remember as a young teacher and now a successful young politician is tragic, more for the country even than yourself.

This was brought home most salutary to us when you appeared on Prime Time to defend that awful letter sent to solicitors acting for autistic children, such deserving members of our 1.053 million families. What is it about this Government that it can be so cruel, particularly to some of the most deserving of our society? Delivering your frightful and frightening message, ostensibly to solicitors but direct to so many suffering families in Ireland, dressed in your usual well-cut suit you stood before the people of Ireland, utterly exposed and utterly heartless.

Election time and you had the effrontery to write looking for our votes and telling us all you had achieved for the constituency. But you didn't have the courage to call. Our paths did cross, however, unexpectedly. It was the third sunday in that extraordinary season of election time and you came to the vigil Mass, not to pray, but to prey, not to accept Christ's message . . . *Take and eat* . . . simply to take, and you didn't even enter the Church, but loitered outside in another of your neatly-tailored suits. Somehow we can't see you loitering outside the Temple of Mammon in Galway but centre stage where neither Christ nor cosmhuintir na hÉireann are welcome. We had occasion in our parish duties to cross the little courtyard. However unexpected, recognition dawned on you and as it did we beheld a sight never to be expected in our lifetime. You, a Government Minister, began to shrink before our eyes, not for anything that was said for no word was. No, it was that little something inside your brain of which Shakespeare reminds us *Thus conscience doth make cowards of us all.* As we entered the sacristy we thought that there may yet be redemption for you, not just in election, but that God and Padre Pio may soften your heart now that you still had a conscience.

We recall writing to you when S. started attending school in Australia even enclosing a photograph of her in her school uniform. She has now finished her first year here in a Gaelscoil. Starting in naoineáin shóisearacha she progressed to naoineáin shinsearacha at Easter. She has twice won Gradam na Gaeilge in her class and will be going into Bliain a hAon next month, le cúnamh Dé. Last year she missed a number of weeks because of having to be in Australia. The coming year will be no different. And the year after and continuing through all of her education. Surely, even without a heart, it behoves the Minister for Education to act in the interests of the child.

Some weeks ago we enjoyed an enormous privilege, a guided tour through the excavations of the original Tuath Dhá Mhíle, soon to be concreted, asphalted or whatever over like so much of value to our nation. But nation doesn't count, only money to a once great party. We have been present in Newgrange, not just once but twice, on the morning of the Winter Solstice and have been blessed on both occasions with a full sunrise. The experience is spiritual and sacred as few are on this earth. And as we were walked and talked through Tuath Dhá Mhíle of almost 4,000 years ago the experience was every bit as real and as sacred. The people who lived here, worked here, died here, these are our people, this is our land, this is our life. Our affinity to people, time and place, of *the mists of twice ten thousand years* was as real as are the current generation of our Teaghlach and our neighbours of over forty years in Cabinteely and Dún Laoghaire. What is life but one long day, as the poet Pádraic Colum told John Bowman on radio. And what in our Teachlach is but a series of days brings us back to the people of Tuath Dhá Mhíle in the heartland of Tipperary. That also is S.'s birthright, heritage and reality every bit as much as are her rights with ours within Teaghlach Uí L…….. under God and Bunreacht na hÉireann. We ask only, Minister, now that you are back in office, that this time, immediately, you will choose to ensure these rights for S. and us. How little that is to ask of our Teachta Dála, former Minister of State for Children and now in your second term as Minister for Education and Science in the richest Government in all of the European Union.

You will find us most appreciative. We are grateful for a smile, a cup of cold water, a word of encouragement, a prayer. You will be doing your bit and your duty in fighting child abuse, now a greater threat to society as was recently announced by the World Health Organisation than AIDS or any other plague you wish to mention. There are those who will say that we are becoming unnecessarily panicky about child sexual abuse. The evidence worldwide is that we have not panicked enough. Look to our own Courts, Minister, or down to the nitty gritty with professionals including teachers with experience in the current response to victims. We must understand child sexual abuse as a problem of national and global importance, not bury our heads in the sand. Not in our jurisdiction. You and your Government colleagues and most of all An Taoiseach have to understand the devastating consequences for victims, their families and the community at large. And we have to understand the how and why of paedophilia: the subtle, bizarre and cruel ways in which seemingly blameless and upright men insidiously cripple the most vulnerable members and minds of our society. We have possessed that understanding for a long time, but have ignored it for far too long. As a former teacher and as Minister for Education you will be aware how well William Shakespeare understood and could convey sexual lust. He might well have been writing of the lusts of a paedophile when he wrote Sonnet 129:

> *Th'expense of spirit in a waste of shame*
> *Is lust in action; and till action, lust*
> *Is perjured, murd'rous, bloody full of blame,*
> *Savage, extreme, rude, cruel, not to trust;*
>
> *Enjoyed no sooner but despised straight:*
> *Past reason hunted; and no sooner had,*
> *Past reason hated, as a swallowed bait,*
> *On purpose laid to make the taker mad:*

Mad in pursuit, and in possession so.
Had, having, and in quest to have, extreme,
A bliss in proof, and proved, a very woe;
Before, a joy proposed; behind, a dream.

All this the world well knows, yet none knows well
To shun the Heaven that leads men to this Hell.

Welcome to Hell, Minister. We've been here for an aeon and you have helped keep us here.

*   *   *

Congratulations for doing what no other Minister for Justice has done before in this State, growing a home-based industry almost from scratch. You knew it wouldn't take money or grants. Those involved had access to money at every corner and every bank branch. Money came to them as easily as it does to the Department of Finance. No, these people just needed time and space to create their own opportunities. Where your dear grandfather, God rest him, only succeeded in frustrating the 1916 Rising, you have succeeded in out-Boycotting Boycott in Mayo, committing an army of An Garda Síochána against the local people as they attempt to protect their families, their homes, their way of life, their heritage, while giving An Garda Síochána, so many of our young men and women, the unenviable task of defending one of the greediest corporate entities in the world as it attempts to force through an unscrupulous and indefensible deal initiated in secret by the only Government Minister of this State to be jailed for corruption. Not alone have An Garda Síochána been damaged but also by their actions and television pictures thereof, their uniform which should be and for long has been for all a cloth of comfort is now for many a cloth of fear. In committing so many fine young Irishmen and women to such contemptible duty you equally afforded further time and space to those chomping at the bit to create their own opportunities. A double whammy as you gave and continued to give them most generously that time and space they so need to build and to grow their wicked industry.

And so Great Crime Unlimited of Ireland (GCUI) was born and now flourishes across the length and breath of the land. There's not an isolated farm or a no reach inlet that hasn't seen activity like never before. GCUI is the envy of the underworld everywhere, with global contacts from Caracas to Kabul. You order, we deliver. You don't pay, we collect. It's a simple philosophy of business but most effective. Why, in no time, Michael, we had out dodged Dodge City. You remember Dodge City, Minister lately, with Errol Flynn fighting all them baddies and Henry Travers (yes, Charlie, Jimmy Stewart's guardian angel in *It's A Wonderful Life*) telling us *what the New York papers are saying: There's no law west of Chicago, and west of Dodge City, no God.* You've brought us to where we can say *the Irish Papers are saying* and mention any city, town or crossroads in place of Chicago and Dodge City. That's quite an achievement, Michael, even if you held the offices at the top of our system of justice and laws for longer than anyone else.

Indeed, we might even have come to you for a recommendation. You see, one of the earliest pieces of advice we were given was accurate and to the point, or to put it another way, short and not so sweet: *Shoot the bastard.* Three words of enormous wisdom and effect. Before you, Herod-like, wash your hands even in private now that you are no longer in public, Michael, let us examine the positives. To shoot the bastard had much to its credit. It was instant, terminal, final, clean and as befits the Fianna Fáil/PD's Government, most economical. Any fool would recognise that ten grand Euro plus a return ticket to Sydney (optional) for an instant, terminal, final and clean resolution to any and all problems was a much better buy than a €100K plus for a morass of interminable, ineffectual and harrowing eighteen months of legal obfuscation without even an approach to a happy or acceptable outcome. You might say *But what of the consequences?* We would say, Minister lately, that as prisoners at the bar nothing that the Australian and/or Irish legal systems could throw at us would be anything other than playtime in comparison to what we have already suffered at the hands of the legal system in Australia. *Yes but* you may say being the barrister you are now again *what of the sentence?* In comparison to all we have and are still suffering from a failed legal system in Sydney, fully supported by you and your erstwhile Government colleagues, Mountjoy, Portlaoise, Thornton Hall and any and all of their equivalents Down Under would be like holiday resorts in comparison to how S., D. and we have been left in our own home of forty-one years. You could liaise with John Howard for a joint appeal to your friend and ally, George W. Bush, to have him lodge us in Guantanamo or, indeed, dropped into Abu Graib and either or both would be a relief from the living hell in which the legal systems of two countries have left us.

So why didn't we act on the advice to shoot the bastard? Simply because there is a greater law than any of this country or of Australia – indeed a law from which almost all man-made laws derive. However unfashionable it is to even refer to it now in Irish public life, it is still there and every bit as real as it ever was. However much we hate the sin, we do not abhor the sinner. Even in trying to understand and love the perpetrator we have all the more got to be alert to the safeguarding and rearing of S.

Child sex abuse culminates in a complex relationship that for the victim is both exploitative and loving, cruel and kind, simple and cunning, perverted and normal all at the same time. Already, although not a cent has been paid towards any maintenance, S. has been promised that there will be a new swimming pool at his brother's house next Christmas and Rudolf the well-known reindeer will be there to meet her.

A hallmark of sexual abuse of children is the use of denial, not only by the offender but by his family, friends, employers, therapists, criminal justice personnel, Government Ministers, and any and every person regardless of rank who protects and gives credence and support to such denial and deception. In denial, all consciously or subconsciously become enablers, allowing the perpetrator to continue his sexual abuse on his victim(s). Perpetrators are the greatest liars and cheats among the whole of the human race. They deny the behaviour itself (*it didn't happen* as has always been his excuse in our case), denial of responsibility for it (some excuse like *it was drink* or *drugs* or as in our case *playing*), denial that any harm was done (*she didn't complain*), denial of the need for any intervention (*I'll never do it again* or as in our case *I know I need help, a lot of professional help* which we offered to arrange but our offer was never taken up). Add to all of these excuses an unlimited range of inducements, promises, threats, bribery and intimidation and you will clearly see that the whole community and your former Department in particular have a huge and active role to play, which to date they have singularly failed to do as they did with the law on Criminal Assault. Does the Department of Justice, Equality and Law Reform have a policy on child abuse? We doubt it. When we found ourselves at the Gates of Hell in Sydney an unsolicited message came through to us from the Department: *If that woman brings that child back to Ireland she will be sent back to Australia and charged with abduction.* Talk about friendly fire in Baghdad or Afghanistan. Such a threat to the mother of a three-year-old child already at the Gates of Hell because of the sexual abuse of her daughter was savagery, we almost said barbarism but that would be unfair to barbarians. We have never heard of any race of people who forcibly by law obliged any mother to hand over her three/four/five/now six-year-old child to the man who was abusing her. Have you, Michael McDowell? Whatever Clintonesque caricature made that comment showed that no such policy exists, that she/he has no knowledge of life and even worse for an official of the Department, no knowledge of Bunreacht na hÉireann and therefore of the legal system in this country.

So where's the policy, Minister lately? Did you listen to the Lord Chancellor across the water earlier this year: *Policy must come first. The law second.* Yet shortly afterwards you were trying to patch another flawed law, trying to close off a legal loophole in child protection law, while maintaining it was a relatively minor matter. In child protection, nothing is a relatively minor matter. The Pharisees forgot that, like policy, people come first.

Notwithstanding taking into account the Extradition Act, 1965, Criminal Law (Jurisdiction) Act 1976, Extradition (European Convention on the Suppression of Terrorism) Act 1987 and Offences Against the State Act 1939, and despite a High Court judgement against him in the matter, the Supreme Court on 13th March, 1990, found for the applicant, Dermot Finucane, against John Paul McMahon, District Justice Peter A. Connellan and The Governor of Portlaoise Prison, allowed his appeal and directed his release, pursuant to Article 40.2° of Bunreacht na hÉireann. Further, in assenting to the judgement, McCarthy J. held that where a citizen objects to his extradition on the grounds that, if delivered to the authorities in the requesting state, he will be ill-treated, the standard of proof which should be required by the Irish courts is whether it has been established that there is a real danger of ill-treatment.

What has happened within the Department of Justice, Equality and Law Reform and to Bunreacht na hÉireann in the intervening seventeen years, for most of which you, Michael, held the two highest legal offices in the State, Attorney General and Minister for Justice, Equality and Law Reform? We did send you, Michael, and An Taoiseach, full details quite a while ago. We received the usual round of useless replies. In case you no longer have access to the file, you'll find full details at your reclaimed place of work, the Law Library, I.I.R. The Irish Report pages 165-227. The basis of the judgement is far more readily available to all citizens except apparently those well-funded and well-privileged by their other co-citizens, we refer, of course, to officials of the Department of Justice, Equality and Law Reform. So let us remind you and them of Article 40.2°:

The State shall, in particular, by its laws protect as best it may from unjust attack and, in the case of injustice done, vindicate the life, person, good name, and property rights of every citizen.	*Déanfaidh an Stát, go sonrach, lena dhlithe, beatha agus pearsa agus dea-chlú agus maoinchearta an uile shaoránaigh a chosaint ar ionsaí éagórach chomh fada lena chumas, agus iad a shuíomh i gcás éagóra.*

. . . *from unjust attack . . . vindicate the life, person . . . rights of every citizen . . . beatha agus pearsa . . . an uile shaoránaigh a chosaint . . .* while we – not only S. – have our lives controlled and pained and devalued by a single terrorist 12,000 miles away, who has the complete and utter support of you, Minister lately, and the Department of Justice, Equality and Law Reform. For this alone you should all hang your heads in shame to think that in cooperating with President Bush by giving him open access to Shannon Airport you are acting against terrorism. We know what terrorism is and we know you have supported rather than opposed or relieved it.

Why, oh why, and how could you ignore such direct, clear and lucid languages over the past two and a half years. Where is the ambiguity? *The State* **shall / Déanfaidh** *an Stát*, every iota as definite as in Article 41, *The State, therefore* **guarantees / Ráthaíonn** *an Stát*. Does anyone in the Department of Justice, Equality and Law Reform even possess a copy of Bunreacht na hÉireann? Does anyone in the Department of Justice, Equality and Law Reform ever read Bunreacht na hÉireann? In either official language? In contrast, Michael, you were the most vociferous, most strident supporter of An Taoiseach in his efforts to elasticise Article 13.6 to, if not beyond, breaking point, as any balanced view of the detailed Articles 12 to 14 relating to An tUachtarán show, to further his own political aim. What an irony that the Irish people are obliged to a foreign Prime Minister in a foreign parliament for keeping our Constitution intact, which Tony Blair did when he stepped back from the joint efforts in relation to letting some 160 paramilitaries go free. If only, Michael, you had been as committed to clear unambiguous Articles to let S., D. and us go free.

Did you, Minister lately, ever realise or indeed anyone in your Department, during all the time you held office, that you were Minister for Justice not of Law? Of course, in Irish, you're title includes the word Dlí, but is immediately and fully balanced by the word Cirt, of Justice, of Right, just what we have claimed for S., D. and our Teaghlach, while you have consistently denied and chosen to ignore our claim. Whatever happened to *Justice delayed is justice denied?*

Even if we turn to consider law, which we shouldn't have to, why, oh why, do you continue with the flawed principle of presumed innocence when there is universal acceptance of its flawlessness. Even in our own lifetime had there been such stulfication of thought, development and reform, we would have no television even in black and white, no electronics, no mobile 'phones. You can follow the same logic through any other profession or business you choose. Add to that even a basic understanding of sex addiction – just as with any other addiction – the utter deceit, deception, denial, cheating, lying, surreptitiousness, cunning, planning both short and long term, subtlety, determination, allure, temptation, and answer how the **presumed** innocence of any such person can outweigh and obliterate the **real** innocence of a three/four/five/six-year-old child? Has the whole Department, along with the Department of Health and Children, sunk so low in a morass of immorality and amorality that they no longer have any concept of childhood innocence? Why else would they toss such innocence into an ocean of lust and evil?

This man acknowledged his sexual depravity and problems and his need for professional help, yet this was disregarded in the Magistrate's Court and the Family Court (sic) of Australia, as being consenting behaviour between adults. What utter tosh. What walk of life other than law sails on magnificently on its Caribbean Cruise on an ocean of lust and evil? Michael Soden, Chief Group Executive of Bank of Ireland was fired for an indiscreet e-mail on his office computer; aircraft manufacturer, Boeing, sacked its President and Chief Executive Officer, Harry Stonecipher, for having an affair with a female executive; the multinational finance services group Merrill Lynch sacked thirteen of its Dublin staff as part of its inquiry into the sending of pornographic e-mails; and the career of one of the world's most respected business leaders crashed to an ignominious end when BP Chief Executive, Lord Browne, had to resign following revelations that he had lied about details of his male lover to a High Court judge in London. At least three of these high flyers neither preyed on nor sought to nor caused any harm to any customer, unlike the man we have to deal with, as per his e-mail . . . *and maybe meet as I do some house calls in* .... Why is the corporate conscience of international business greater than that of the Department of Justice, Equality and Law Reform? Why is there not at least a comparable level of ethics within the richest Government in the European Union? Why did Peter Sutherland fight for several years to limit any damage Lord Browne's personal life could inflict on his company's reputation and not one, repeat Minister lately, not one of the Cabinet in which you served, not one in the Department which you headed, or in any other department made any effort to limit or contain the damage this man's personal life has inflicted and continues to inflict on this Teaghlach, including S. and her beloved mother?

We repeat, Minister lately, our man can even make an asset of his work in pursuit of sex as he sets his mind and his lure on his next victim, *Hi, got your message from pinkboard and maybe meet as I do some house calls in* .... How many, Michael, of the 2.106 million parents of families in Ireland would be happy to have such a man have access to their home and families just to fix their kitchen appliances? Would you and Mrs McDowell?

We won't go into the full detail of some twenty visits to the above-named courts – you've received all details already. We'll just remind you of four. How at the very outset Legal Aid told us sorry we've corrupted (their word, not ours) ourselves and can't act for you. And how at a most critical stage of our efforts to safeguard S. the learned Judge found against us on the basis that she could not accept that the alleged actions could happen in a public place in the light of day. Some ten days later a lad of seventeen years was shot dead in an amusement centre at three o'clock in the afternoon within a quarter of a mile of the Judge's court. No doubt, with the same twisted illogicality, the learned Judge visited the grieving parents and returned their son Lazarus-like to them on the basis that the killing could not have happened in a public place in the light of day.

In the Family (sic) Court of Australia another learned Judge in her decision opted for a psychologist at Aus$6,000 rather than a psychologist at Aus$3,000 to prepare a report for the Final Hearing six weeks hence. Money up front, of course, fulfilling the two guiding principles of family law in Australia, make it as expensive as possible and get the money in first. People don't matter and children don't exist. As the eminent, more truthfully costly, psychologist obviously believed, too. For such money and for such a crucial service to the Family (sic) Court the least one should expect of such a specialist is that his choice of premises and staff should be in keeping with, and reflect his appreciation of, his work. A little garden suitably furnished, a play area however modest, an understanding child carer if not a child nurse, as a minimum towards being child friendly. But not for this Family (sic) Court appointed specialist whose report was going to be so critical in the decision for life of our dear granddaughter. His office/room was on the seventh floor of a glass block, furnished, we thought, with little if any acknowledgement to any child being assessed but more of an 1800's gentleman's club in London – with a waiting area, which doubled as reception, so narrow that if two people sat in the two chairs facing one another they would first need to seriously negotiate knee and leg room to avoid either rather painful injury or the accusation of indulging in Kama Sutra therapy. There was, of course, no child-minder nor nurse nor any member of staff to care for S. so that when the eminent Family (sic) Court appointed specialist was having his one to one interview with D. about all those adult personal matters he was to enquire into, it was a one to one to one interview as S. was ensconced on the one place available and acceptable to her, her mother's knee. Need we say more of basic facilities. For a hugely less fee there are hugely more facilities for S. and the children of our neighbourhood when we visit our child-friendly and more than competent family doctor in Cabinteely. As to the eminent, Court-appointed specialists report, you are welcome to invite us to discuss it over coffee in the Law Library at your convenience but we will have so much to say against it that you should include lunch and probably dinner as well in your invitation.

Our fourth and final comment to you on the Courts. The Final Hearing was set for an almost unprecedented seven days at the request of the other party as he tried to further intimidate us by costs.

He didn't. The dates were scheduled some six months in advance, to begin on the Feast of St. Anthony, 13th June. As late as the final days of April this schedule was confirmed by the learned Judge in the Family (sic) Court of Australia. All our planning, finance, travel and any and all other arrangements for ourselves, our witnesses in Ireland, our witnesses in Australia, our legal team, our care for S., all had been set for a seven day hearing starting on 13th June, including those who had to rearrange holidays already booked and/or forego their June break. Then without warning or consultation an overnight bombshell by e-mail to inform us that the dates had been vacated – a somewhat crude and cruel term in the circumstances. Leaving aside the discourtesy and ill-consideration to all the adults – family, witnesses and legal team – involved, what utter disservice, negligence and deprivation to S.'s future and life. It was as if the child who should have been the heart, the centre, the focus of all that had gone on through eighteen months of the legal process did not matter, even worse, did not exist. It was the final confirmation that the Family (sic) Court of Australia knew nothing of, cared nothing for, the beautiful, innocent, little girl that it would purport to have an interest in, a responsibility to and yet would so arrogantly brush aside in its own interest, selfishness and indifference.

None of this is news to you, Minister lately. We informed you while you were still in office, and An Taoiseach, and each member of Government of these facts as they occurred, indeed, pointing out to you and your colleagues in Cabinet that Saddam Hussein at that same time for all his crimes against humanity was being accorded greater respect and being treated with greater dignity in the International Court of Justice in the Hague than was our daughter in the Magistrate and Family (sic) Courts in Australia. It is to the eternal shame of the Government in which you were Minister for Justice, Equality and Law Reform that no action, legal, diplomatic or otherwise was taken in relation to our situation. What an utter dereliction and neglect of both Bunreacht na hÉireann and the sovereignty proclaimed under arms by the men and women of 1916 and again affirmed in the opening article of that same Bunreacht na hÉireann:

Article 1	Airteagal 1
The Irish Nation hereby affirms its inalienable, indefeasible, and sovereign right to choose its own form of Government, to determine its relations with other nations, and to develop its life, political, economic and cultural, in accordance with its own genius and traditions.	Deimhníonn náisiún na hÉireann leis seo a gceart doshannta, dochloíte, ceannasach chun cibé cineál Rialtais is rogha leo féin a bhunú, chun a gcaidreamh le náisiúin eile a chinneadh, agus chun a saol polaitíochta is geilleagair is saíochta a chur ar aghaidh de réir dhúchais is gnás a sinsear.

Do none of The Articles of The Universal Declaration of Human Rights apply in Ireland or in Australia?

Just tell us please, Minister lately, you of the enviable reputation as a barrister and with ten years in the two top posts of Justice in this State, who in the whole area of law in this State and /or in Australia cares one whit for our S., her life and her welfare on a day-to-day basis? Who loves her enough to care for her, to provide a home for her, to feed her, to clothe her, to see to her education, her health, her fun, her sports, her development, her creativity and every good aspect of her life on a **daily** basis seven days a week from breakfast to breakfast to breakfast? In the short-term? In the long-term? Do tell us please, Michael, what Minister for Justice, Equality and Law Reform, what departmental Secretary General or official, what learned Judge, what Attorney General in either or both jurisdictions will be around for S., even be aware of her, in twenty years time? Courts are set up for the people and not *vice versa*. When that swing begins, justice is no longer only blind but dodgy and democracy is teetering on the brink.

The man who sought and was given a seven-day hearing has been an insidious canker in our family for over ten years. He has subjected our daughter to a decade of domestic violence, financial control, threats and unspeakable terror, with all the concomitant anguish and harm to S., D. and us. Further he has been enabled to continue to do so by the total support of two governments – Australian and Irish –

while we have been denied protection from either. In contrast, you and your Department have a law to protect a pair of panties hanging on a clothesline in Waterford. You think so highly of that law that you invoked and pursued it to the letter against one of your own, a member of An Garda Síochána. Do tell us please, Minister lately, how a pair of panties, however clean, can have greater constitutional protection than an Irish family? Not just us, but we're sure that each and every one of the 1.053 million families in Ireland would like to know also.

We might say that on our experience whoever said that The Law is an ass was grossly unfair to the ass. But we don't. However, it is risibly tragic and tragically risible that the welfare, wellbeing and indeed life of a three and a half now six year old child should be sacrificed on some iconoclastic altar without the semblance of either reason or common sense. Here is a man of such admitted perversity and perfidy whose gross admitted sexual acts and deviancy are set aside by the Magistrates Court and the Family (sic) Court of Australia as being acceptable behaviour between consenting adults and having thus cleansed, sanitised and canonised him view him now as a model human being to whom even the thought not to mention the whiff of child sexual abuse cannot attach. How rightly and visibly should those intimidating words of Dante Alighieri be carved above the entrance to any and all courts of Magistrates and Family (sic) in Australia: *Abandon hope all you innocent who enter here*. The *innocent* is our interjection. And you, Minister lately, and all of your Cabinet colleagues including An Taoiseach and Uachtarán na hÉireann gave and continue to give your unswerving loyalty to such damnable action against the innocence of our beautiful granddaughter, her equally innocent mother, and we their Irish family. How can anyone of you look at yourself in a mirror, lie comfortable in bed at night or ride about in the plushness of a State car provided on the backs of so many of the families of Ireland. How could justice and politics sink so low in this State? Jonathan Swift wrote *Real vision is the ability to see the invisible*. Sometimes real vision is the ability to see the obvious.

Or are we to rely solely on the words of St. Paul *For the truth about* us will be brought out in the law court of Christ, and each of us will get what he deserves for the things he did in the body, good or bad (2 Cor. 5.10)?

On your departure from politics, you declared your love for Ireland. What Ireland, Michael? The mountains, the waterways (unpolluted, polluted?), the grass in your back garden? Remember, James Larkin declared that *Ireland without its people means nothing to me*. What do we mean to you? What do 1.053 million families mean to you and to the Department of Justice, Equality and Law Reform? Regrettably, the words of William Shakespeare still hold true, *The evil that men do lives after them*. Because of your neglect, your omission, your choice to ignore us, our evil still lives with us.

Now you have been succeeded as Minister for Justice, Equality and Law Reform by Brian Lenihan, a man who in his previous role as Minister of State for Children with a seat at the cabinet table, chose neither to meet us nor to act for S., D. or us. How tragic. We knew his father, a friendly man, walked O'Connell Street with him, wined and dined with him in the Shelbourne Hotel and in the Shamrock Lodge. He didn't deserve to be treated like he was by Fianna Fáil. No more than we do by the Department which his son now heads nor by the Government in which his son now serves. Will he now do what you chose not to do and give us the protection Bunreacht na hÉireann guarantees to us and to all Irish teaghlaigh?

*   *   *

Before Martin Cullen was, we are. Born and reared on the Quay looking out on the magnificence of the Suir, then a quality river with far cleaner water flowing to the sea than there is now. Close to the Bridge that dominated our childhood and early dreams. The Bridge, not the present structure, but the son of old Timbertoes. Gateway to the world, to Kilkenny, Wexford, Thurles, Limerick, even the metropolis itself, Dublin. Return entrance to our own city and to home. Even when we heard of those great bridges of the world, O'Connell, Tower, Tiber, Brooklyn, Golden Gate and Sydney

Harbour, they had to stand in line to ours. It was after all The Bridge. Now that we've seen all those and more, it is still The Bridge, gateway to childhood and growing up, to family and to friends long gone, to love and fun and tragedy, to enrichment of life, to learning and experience, to roots and belonging and knowing who we are.

The Bridge, the link to two worlds of adventure. The Knock across the river, slightly foreign being Kilkenny. The railway station where the trains from Rosslare, Limerick Junction and Dublin puffed and shuddered to a halt. Sallypark, a lovely homely village, now gone, sacrificed to progress. The stony steps that lifted us to the skies and to the top of the Knock where wild gorse and rocks made a child's playground, unlimited and free. The Golf Course where occasionally we were blessed to be called to caddy and to return home tired but with sixpence triumphant in our trousers' pocket. Riches, for we that had little appreciated little. Perched on the hill stood the Bishop's Palace, looking down on the great river and across at the city like a benign custodian, behind whose back we sometimes ventured to the Yorkshire Road and home by Ferrybank.

The Rock, on our home side of the river, our always friend yet slightly intimidating for the bluster of life seemed to end at The Bridge and up beyond it was somehow not just quieter but lonelier, bordering on eerie. Cherry's Brewery, then on to the foundry full of mystery, where the river bank opened up to present a place of play and water, a good but dangerous combination. Further up, the Red Bridge appropriately named and coloured for the trains to Cork. That was another country. The Red Bridge, so sturdy, so expansive, and when we finally plucked up the courage to climb up the steep embankment, so open. Our surprise so great we nearly fell through the iron trellis work.

Bridge Street, with the Arcade and Murphy's and the sweetness of the Green Bank. Further up the waft of O'Brien's Bakery and the sounds and dust of Morris's coal yard before the street split its mind between The Glen and Gracedieu. Closer to the Quay, O'Connell Street cut away between the Dominican Church and Breen's huge emporium, God and Mammon, a prophetic oracle of an Ireland yet to come. Kenneally's stores and Croker's reaching to Denny's Lane that was really Penrose Lane, later to lend its name to Penrose Crystal.

Holding the corner was Bowe's butcher shop with Murphy's hackney and Kavanagh's enterprising electric shop, for electricity still had its magic of newness and rural electrification had yet to be talked about. George White & Sons pharmacy gave *éclat* to the street as the presses of The Waterford News – long before The Waterford Star reached the city – rattled out the news of the day in competition with The Munster Express's news of the week and its upmarket standing with a special Kilkenny edition. Further on, Dee's and Meagher's and the Chamber of Commerce and the Presbyteries and Toolans even then a special place rushed O'Connell Street into the narrow confines of George's Street before the city broke into the expanse of the aptly named The Cross and Broad Street, the city's bazaar, where all human life came to shop and to gaze. Dominating Barronstrand Street from behind its great railings now long gone, the Cathedral of the Most Holy Trinity Without drew the rich and the poor, the saint and the sinner, to pray and to worship the one true God. There, on the stroke of twelve o'clock on Christmas Eve night, a real midnight Mass began with all the delight and solemnity and joy of that sacred festival. Bells and *O Holy Night* rang out so clearly and incense rose from the sanctuary to fill the vast reaches of the Cathedral with Stanley Bowyer at the organ in the gallery and His Lordship, Dr. Daniel Cohalan from Cork preaching at the altar. From here, on Corpus Christi, the huge procession set out with prayers and hymns towards the Clock Tower, turning right along the Quay, into the Mall and Parnell Street and Manor Street, a moving stream of people of all ages, ascending Bunker's Hill for the higher expanse of the city to come to the reverence and the climax of Benediction on the Hill of Ballybricken, all under the direction and stentorian voice of Fr. Farrell. A man twice blessed, for it was he also who organised the annual carnival, that hub of innocent enjoyment for young and old, in the Barracks on the profits of which the new parish of the Holy Family gained its new church. Ballybricken, with its fabled bullpost, hosted the fairs of cattle and pigs and farmers and dealers from home and far-flung borders of neighbouring counties, with the Yellow Road as ever, like Dorothy's Yellow Brick Road, running away *Over the Rainbow* to reach the Mercy Convent, where the most gentle woman ever to take a veil in the service of Christ, Sister Anthony, known to all as Mother Anthony, took the care, education, formation and destiny of so many of the young boys of four into her hands until they reached the ripe old age of First Communion.

Before her first birthday, Martin Cullen, we introduced S. to this, her heritage and her lineage, and much more. To Colbeck Street and resonances of Waterford's now paled fame on the concert stages of the world from London to Australia to South America, the United States and back to London, of Wallace's then great hit, Maritana, whose *I dreamt I dwelt in Marble Halls* was a favourite at family gatherings in the city by the Suir. We didn't trouble you then because we had no need to – more true, because we were not yet aware we had a need to. But we did, along with all your other Ministerial colleagues when we became aware and you gave us the deaf ear. Ignored each and every plea we made. Could you not, as Minister for Transport, be moved by the pain and anguish caused by every plane and jet that traversed the sky over Sydney each telling D. in her hostaged captivity that you can't fly with us, you can't have the freedom of all others, including your persecutor, to travel as you choose, you can't take S. home to Ireland. Could you not hear S.'s little voice ask so often why can't we go in an aeroplane again? To Ireland, to Mamó and Daideo, to her uncles and aunts and cousins whom she so loved? Could you not feel the heartbreak and heartwrenching of Sydney Airport departures for D. as we, her family, her mother, her father, her brother, her cousins and friends, shook with tears at long goodbyes that might well have been our last. We have stood at tragic gravesides where such depths of emotion were not plunged. But the man of Waterford at the Cabinet table chose to ignore us. The man of Waterford whose knowledge of history is such that he removed the Franciscan, Luke Wadding, from his fifty-year stand on a plinth as the Quay cedes into the Mall to be replaced by a statue of Thomas Francis Meagher for the occasion of a European Union shindig without realising that however worthy of the honour of a statue in his home city Meagher is, he was no European, but a staunch Irishman whose international contribution was to the United States of America while Wadding – the originator of Waterford's lovely appellation of *parva Roma* – was one of the most distinguished of that small band of Irishmen, pre-European Union, who were distinctly and deservedly European in career, outlook, achievement and stature, equally at home in his Franciscan cell and in the Papal and Royal Courts of his time. Yes, Minister Cullen, you are the man who stood at the centre of the new bridge and threw €60 million of the Waste Fund for drop dead electronic voting machines down the Swanee, pardon us, the Suir, declaring to those gathered along the banks as their money floated to the sea before their eyes, *Don't worry, folks, we'll still get value for it. And come back next year and the year after ad infinitum and I'll toss in another €1 million or so on wasted storage.* Tossing the €60 million over the parapet at the rate of €1,000 per minute (pretty good going for any Minister) it would take you, Minister Cullen, 42 days working 24 hours per day to complete the task. Just think, the whole of Lent with Pancake Tuesday and Easter Monday thrown in. Of course if you were to do likewise with the National Roads Authority's fabulous overrun you'd need to outlive Methusaleth and even our grandchildren to the nth generation wouldn't see you complete the task. How S. and so many of the children of this State could benefit from such largesse properly applied.

You are the Minister who held up the National Roads Authority as an example on timing and budgeting to the whole of the European Union overlooking that just two short years ago it was guilty of the greatest overrun ever in this State and probably ever in most, if not all, of the member states. Eight to twelve billion Euro depending on which source one believes – the Authority itself admits to eight. The scale is so vast that it is mind-blowing. That's largesse at a level that should have funded solutions to all the shortcomings of this Government for this generation and probably future generations of Irish children, including S.

But Martin Cullen, Minister for Transport, now Minister for Social and Family Affairs (how Family, Minister?) chose not to hear, chose not to help. S. has enjoyed other visits to Waterford since, to her family and extended family. She will continue to do so and as a young woman will cross Edmund Ignatius Rice Bridge blissfully unaware of Martin Cullen the Minister from Waterford who could, should, have done so much for her but chose not to. And she will move down the Quay with a spring in her step, past where we were born and reared, in the full freedom of a citizen of this State, however we achieve it, but regrettably, with no thanks to Martin Cullen, Minister now for Social and Family (sic) Affairs.

* * *

Among your Cabinet, a Thaoisigh, there are two who made a positive though limited effort on our behalf, to whom we are most grateful and offer our appreciation. The first is Micheál Ó Máirtín, Minister for Enterprise, Trade and Employment. Head and shoulders above all other members of the Cabinet including yourself, a Thaoisigh, Minister Ó Máirtín agreed to meet, did meet us, gave us a commitment and honoured his commitment. He met us on a night when we considered he would be too busy to give us much of a hearing, the opening night of a new Dáil year. He gave us a full and generous hearing, *as Gaeilge*. We were most impressed, but then he is the first and only minister to match the scale and audacity of Donagh O'Malley's political stroke. For what O'Malley did for the education of the people of Ireland, in taking cigarettes out of the pubs, restaurants, offices and public buildings of our State, Ó Máirtín has done for the health of the nation. He has set an international domino for good in motion. As we write we learn that Finland is the latest country to follow his lead. His place in history is assured for if we may extemporise on the words of the Magnificat *From now on all generations will call him blessed*. Minister Ó Máirtín undertook to make what representations he could on our behalf. We believe that he did because he made good on his other promise, that on his forthcoming trip to Sydney he would meet S. and D. That simple meeting, so much in contrast to Brian Cowan's rebuff, was a relief, an uplift, a positive in an unrelieving horror and an acknowledgement that someone in the Irish Government cared. How valuable and essential is a cup of cold water in a drought. It may not rank with the ban on smoking, but that simple act of compassion will be remembered and cherished in this Teaghlach and S. will be made aware of it in years to come. Go raibh maith agat, a Aire.

The second is Mary Coughlan, Minister for Agriculture and Food, who wrote that letter to which we have already referred, dated 5th May 2006, coincidentally S.'s fifth birthday. As a member of Government, Minister Coughlan's acknowledgment that *once that Court decision has been made, the Department of Foreign Affairs and the Irish State can institute, if necessary, protection arising out of the Court decision*, was seminal, monumental and redemptive not alone for its content but also for its timing. We were at a very low ebb after almost eighteen months of an extended *annus horribilis* which was far longer then any Roman or, indeed, Queen Elizabeth II would believe a year could be. In truth, any *annus horribilis* is eternal to those who suffer through it. Your letter was a godsend, Minister, and a *consolation devoutly to be wished for*. It was more. It was a bedrock, a benchmark and a defence against the constant demands made on and of us as we negotiated conditions under which we could be allowed to take S. to the love and care and protection awaiting her in Ireland. The love and care she has in abundance. But the protection has never materialised, indeed, has been denied. Why, Minister Coughlan? Perhaps more apposite, why, a Thaoisigh?

* * *

de hÍde, Ó Ceallaigh, de Valéra, Childers, Ó Dálaigh, Hillery, Robinson . . . For S., no garden party, no candle in the window, no welcome at the door, no fáilte isteach, no step along the corridor, no sinking in the soft deep pile of the Donegal carpet, no handshake, no salutation, no tea and biscuits, no biscuits, no tea, no support, no intervention, no Bunreacht na hÉireann, no rights, no protection, freedom is eternal, S. is six.

Jesus wept. We've been to the Church of the Tear. We know why Jesus wept over Jerusalem. We understand how he could have wept over Auschwitz and Belsen. We can comprehend why he would weep over Iraq. Why he would weep over Áras an Uachtaráin we find incomprehensible. Why he should weep over Áras an Uachtaráin with a Giolla Íosa in residence we find unbelievable. But then we remember that He was the man who put children at the centre of life and of his teaching. Mark (9.36-37) tells us *He took a little child and had her stand among them. Taking her in his arms, he said to them, Whoever welcomes one of these little children in my name welcomes me.* And in the next chapter (10.14) *Let the little children come to me, and do not hinder them, for the Kingdom of God belongs to such as these.* Matthew, too, carried the same message but also records the admonition *See that you do not look down on one of these little ones. For I tell you that their angels in Heaven always see the face of my Father in heaven* (18.10). Matthew is also the evangelist who records Jesus' dire warning of *a large millstone hung around his neck and be drowned in the depths of the sea* (18.6) – repeated in Mark 9.42 – and the precept *In the same way your Father in Heaven is not willing that any of these should be lost* (Mt 18.14). Remembering these words we come to understand the incomprehensible, that Jesus wept and weeps over Áras an Uachtaráin today. For in how S. has been treated, despised, neglected and humbled, and we her Teaghlach too, we find resonance and understanding and hope in the words *whoever humbles himself like this child* (our S.) *is the greatest in the Kingdom of Heaven* (Mt 18.4).

We are not so naïve as to think that the words of Jesus Christ are accepted in this State as broadly as they so recently were. That does not diminish them for us. Our beloved Sugarloaf does not go away every or any time it is covered in mist. Seeing isn't always believing as the Apostle Thomas found out. But we would have thought that you, a Uachtaráin, would still believe, given your faith, your background and that you were the choice of Cardinal and Bishops before ever Charlie Haughey and Fianna Fáil showed interest in you. Indeed, it was probably being the preferred of the Hierarchy that was your springboard to politics. The office of Uachtaráin is supposed to be above politics and generally has been. Paddy Hillery was challenged very adamantly to protect that independence and integrity and Cearbhall Ó Dálaigh before him resigned to defend them. So you will understand if we challenge your stated reasons for leaving S., D. and us to a fate worse than death. You gave them to us twice, appropriately in both official languages:

I am afraid that it would not be appropriate for the President, in view of the constitutional requirements of her office to intervene.	*ní miste dom a mhíniú duit go bhfuil an tUachtarán srianta ag cúinsí bunreachtúla a hoifige. Is é is brí leis seo nach bhfuil sí in ann a ladar a chur isteach i scéal ar bith a thagann faoi údarás an rialtais nó na gcúirteanna.*

You have twice successfully offered yourself for election, are now in your second term, have a first-class facility in both official languages, and so must have full cognisance of the import and standing of the declaration of office, the only such declaration in Bunreacht na hÉireann, which you have given to the Irish people at two inaugurations:

"In the presence of Almighty God I do solemnly and sincerely promise and declare that I will maintain the Constitution of Ireland and uphold its laws, that I will fulfil my duties faithfully and conscientiously in accordance with the Constitution and the law, and that I will dedicate my abilities to the service and welfare of the people of Ireland. May God direct and sustain me."	"I láthair Dia na nUilechumhacht, táimse á ghealladh agus á dhearbhú go sollúnta is go fírinneach bheith i mo thaca agus i mo dhídin do Bhunreacht Éireann, agus a dlíthe a chaomhnú, mo dhualgais a chomhlíonadh go dílis coinsiasach de réir an Bhunreacht is an dlí, agus mo lándícheall a dhéanamh ar son leasa is fónaimh mhuintir na hÉireann. Dia do mo stiúradh agus do mo chumhdach."

This declaration clearly, as should be, sets (a) the Constitution in prime position (*maintain/bheith i mo thaca agus i mo dhídin do*) over the laws, (b) the Constitution in prime position before the law following *I will fulfil my duties faithfully and conscientiously/mo dhualgas a chomhlíonadh go dílis coinsiasach.* (c) finishes with the solemn and sincere promise *that I will dedicate my abilities to the service and welfare of the people of Ireland/mo lándícheall a dhéanamh ar son leasa is fónaimh mhuintir na hÉireann,* which we believe we have more than amply shown includes S., D. and all of Teaghlach Uí L......... (d) carries no condition or sub-clause in relation to the Government/An Rialtas which is not even mentioned.

The stated reasons for leaving us to a fate worse than death then can be based only on Article 13.9:

The powers and functions conferred on the President by this Constitution shall be exercisable and performable by him only on the advice of the Government, save where it is provided by this Constitution that he shall act in his absolute discretion or after consultation with or in relation to the Council of State, or on the advice or nomination of, or on receipt of any other communication from, any other person or body.	*Taobh amuigh de chás dá socraítear leis an mBunreacht seo go ngníomhóidh an tUachtarán as a chomhairle féin, nó tar éis comhairle a ghlacadh leis an gComhairle Stáit, nó go ngníomhóidh sé i dtaobh ní a bhaineas leis an gComhairle Stáit, nó ar chomhairle nó ainmniú aon duine nó aon dreama eile, nó ar aon scéala eile a fháil ó aon duine nó aon dream eile, is ar chomhairle an Rialtais amháin is cead don Uachtarán na cumhachtaí agus na feidhmeanna a bheirtear dó leis an mBunreacht seo a oibriú is a chomhlionadh.*

Article 13.9 does however contain a very precise and important qualification to, indeed exclusion from Government control:

save where it is provided by this Constitution that he shall act in his absolute discretion or after consultation with or in relation to the Council of State, or on the advice or nomination of, or on receipt of any other communication from, **any other person** *or body.*	*taobh amuigh de chás dá socraítear leis an mBunreacht seo go ngníomhóidh an tUachtarán as a chomhairle féin… nó go ngníomhóidh sé i dtaobh ní a bhaineas leis an gComhairle Stáit, nó ar chomhairle nó ainmniú aon duine nó aon dreama eile, nó ar aon scéala eile a fháil* **ó aon duine** *nó aon dream* **eile.**

This most vital stipulation in relation *inter alia* to *any other person/ó aon duine eile*, allied to the declaration of office not only allows but obliges An tUachtarán to act not only in the service and interest of the people of Ireland but in relation to the Constitutional rights we have set out, applicable not alone to S., D. and all of Teachlach Uí L........ but to each and all of the 1.053 million families in this State, of whom we would respectfully remind you, a Uachtaráin, Teaghlach Mhic Ghiolla Íosa is one. Such is far more sound and tenable than the proposal so stridently propounded in Autumn 2005 by An Taoiseach, Bertie Ahern T.D., vociferously supported by, among others, Michael McDowell, T.D., Minister for Justice, Equality and Law Reform, to have you award pardons to IRA members, wanted for paramilitary crimes in the State, under Article 13.6 of the Constitution. Such powers under this Article are vested in you, with no specification that you use them on the instructions of the Government/An Rialtas. On the contrary, the second part of the Article sets out an approach quite separate, i.e. that these powers *may, except in capital cases, also be conferred by law on other authorities*. In including such a proviso, but yet excluding *in capital cases* it is clear that the Constitution provides that such powers are in *his absolute discretion/as a chomhairle féin* as set out in Article 13.9 above. To argue otherwise, is certainly less sound and less tenable than our argument in relation to your declaration of office. How right the Department of Justice's spokeswoman was when she said *But the right to pardon is not delegatable under the Constitution*, Irish Times, November 11, 2005.

Now, on 30th August 2007, we are still living a fate worse than death and praying that you will look afresh at our case for the sake of S. and D. to whom all our efforts, support and love are directed, as should your attention and support be as per your Constitutional declaration to the Irish people on twice taking office.

* * *

Luke, the gentle one. Luke, the educated one. Luke, the doctor. Luke, the healer. Luke, the man of sensitivity. Luke, the man of

Greek culture. Luke, the Jew opening our minds to a new reality. Luke, the man of precision. Luke, the only Evangelist to give us knowledge of Christ sweating blood – *haematidrosis*. Luke, the writer of compassion, whose Gospel has been called *the most beautiful book ever written*. Luke, who gave us the invaluable story of the early church in the Acts of the Apostles. Luke, the man of honesty and integrity who set out his intentions plain from the beginning. *Therefore, since I myself have carefully investigated everything from the beginning, it seemed good also to me to write an orderly account for you* (Lk 1.3). Luke, who might well have been writing to any one of our Tribunals.

This is the man whose name you chose, Bertie Ahern, to use if not abuse for your den of intrigue if not of iniquity. A house of shades and shadows, of mystery and tricks, of the unreal, the appearing, the disappearing, where monies slip and slide in sleight-of-hand and cronyism is brought to state of the art nepotism to out-Quill Quill who declared *We don't believe in nepotism here we only practise it*. A house as Hamlet said from *whose bourne no traveller returns* for we sent a copy of every letter and report to St. Luke's, never to receive a reply.

Yet St. Luke's is real. It exists. It is like a poor man's *Chateau Charvet* based on the same principles if not the grand scale of your political promoter and mentor. It is a prime asset at the heart of your Constituency, a most valuable property, a significant benefit-in-kind (taxable or tax-deductible?), provided by those shadowy characters who somehow always seem to surround you. Do you attract them, Bertie, or do they attract you? Most ideal of all, is the attraction mutual, a kind of never-ending story of love in the style of what's good for me is good for you? Would the book be a romance or a who dunnit? It should be the hub, at best, of Drumcondra, but through your machinations you have made it the hub of the State, rivalling if not surpassing, your office in Government Buildings. Allied to the transitory Temple you raise each year to Mammon, you have created a new Being, a new development in godhead and theology, a Gemini God in which Mammon and Fianna Fáil so fuse that no one, least of all anyone in Fianna Fáil, knows where one begins and the other ends. We are all too well aware of the billions of litres of water this new Gemini God of Mammon and Fianna Fáil has destroyed and polluted throughout the State. Tell us, a Thaoisigh, when will you show us the miracle, even a small one, say, Mammon and Fianna Fáil creating just one litre of **fresh** water? You are the Aaron of the Irish people leading us to a false God, a false dawn and a false life. It is Ireland's tragedy that neither in Church nor State is there a Moses to return us to reality and righteousness.

St. Luke's should, in particular, be irrelevant to us, but it isn't. We came there to find the man of the people but were disappointed. We came there for support but found none. We came there for relief but got none. We came there for action and were ignored. No letter, no word, no acknowledgement of our existence. All this from the man of the people, the man who cares, the presser of the flesh, the common man. An innocent child of three, yet no response. An innocent child of four, yet no response. An innocent child of five, still no response. An innocent child of . . . birthday dawns on fifth of May 2007. S. wakes at ten minutes to seven, looks out her bedroom window into her field of dreams for magically overnight her wish for a trampoline has come true and it now stands in our garden in the early morning sunshine for her cousins and friends to gather round and bounce and spring with such delight that their innocent shrieks and laughter reached all the way to Government Buildings and Drumcondra, but there were *no ears to hear*. That day dawned for you and Brian Cowan lying in the gutter of dig-outs while Michael MacDowell prevaricated to his political doom, vacillating like a dying wasp wondering whether to sting or suck, as to whether to believe you, to back you or not. And the children play and blow out the candles. *He who has ears to hear, let him hear.* (Lk 8.8).

And all the while an innocent mother calls to you, no response. An innocent citizen, no response. An innocent, suffering, agonising mother and citizen, no response. For the man of the people, the man who cares, the presser of the flesh, the common man doesn't exist, is but a myth, a shadow, a shade.

We wrote to you to say we understood, of course Cecilia and Georgina should have their education and that S. and D. should have their freedom. Was that too much to ask for?

And yet, at that time you held the top Ministry in the State, a commanding salary, the best of perks and pension, a top of the range car and a team of drivers, the best seats wherever you chose to go, support of your Government colleagues, unlimited access to the high and the mighty from finance to psychology, all in your own home town with open and ready access to your own circle of family and friends. In contrast, we were 12,000 miles from home, in an hostile and heartless environment of flawed social and legal systems, entrapped by a predatory bisexual sex addict who was already abusing S., with little resources, no perks, being persecuted by one government and abandoned by another. Yet we could reach out to you and you chose to ignore us. Poor us. Poor St. Luke, the man of detail, the only one to record that Christ sweated blood. And he gives the Good Samaritan parable in full, ending with Christ's exhortation *Go and do likewise* (Luke 10.37). That's all we've ever asked that you be Taoiseach and neighbour to S., D. and us.

*   *   *

In the past two years alone, a Thaoisigh, you and your Government have spent €120 billion of our, the people of Ireland's, money. Yet many of our children are starting out in or returning to sub-standard schools while others cannot even get a place. Children are still put into adult psychiatric wards; children across the wide range of diseases are left without adequate care and continue to be denied the best chances of being prepared for life. Many are going to bed hungry, that is if they have a bed. Drugs and alcohol and excess and binge drinking by our young are almost out of control; and now we hear that children as young as six and many between six and eleven are opting for self-harm while we are top of the league for young suicides. What malaise is running rampant side by side and often intermingled with wealth through the society over which you have presided for the past ten years? These are our children, our future, the hope of this country for the next generation and you have abandoned them as you have S. We have been trying to get your attention for S. for over two and a half years. Why do you continue to choose to ignore us? Is it too much to expect of the richest Government in Europe that S. and D. should enjoy freedom, freedom from abuse, freedom from threats, freedom from fear? How can you, a Thaoisigh, continue to shirk your Constitutional duty to provide protection to S., to D. and to us? Is that too much for us to ask after over one hundred and twenty years of loyal citizenship?

Throughout your whole period in office, a Thaoisigh, you have talked persistently of the economy and its close relation economics. Neither word appears in Bunreacht na hÉireann. The adjective *economic* does once in Article 1, which affirms the right of the Irish nation *inter alia;*

to develop its life, political, economic and cultural, in accordance with its own genius	*chun a saol polaitíochta is geilleagair is saíochta a chur ar aghaidh de réir dhúchais is gnás a sinsear.*

But *Personal Rights / Cearta Pearsanta* and *The Family / An Teaghlach* do. They even have a sub-section each under the heading *Fundamental Rights / Bunchearta*.

Compassion, like mercy, is twice-blessed. It is not a burden on the economy. It costs nothing. Like kindness, it is a language which the deaf can hear and the blind can see. Yet with the one great exception of Anne Webster, and Mícheál Ó Máirtín to a lesser extent, compassion has been absent across the whole of your Government and administration. You surrounded yourself with four women to each of whom you gave considerable power. Four Marys – Harney, Hanafin, Coughlan and McAleese – each named after the Mother of God and not an iota of compassion or Constitutional care between them. It says so much about your administration, your republicanism, your socialism, your humanity and about yourself. Surely there must be someone among your array of Ministers, civil servants and advisers that, like the Centurion, you can turn to and say *'Do this', and he does it.* (Lk 7.8).

Surely you must value 1.053 million families that much. Surely you must value Teaghlach Uí L........ that much. What value do you, a Thaoisigh, put on one Irish life? Your erstwhile visitor, Mr. John Howard, shortly before he came to Ireland gave this valuation of his own people *All the gold in Australia is not worth one Australian life.* Surely an Irish life is equally valuable. And if so, why do you choose to let us languish in our horror? Had a dingo been as maltreated in Ireland as we have been in Australia there would have been uproar at both ends of the world. Must we, to receive justice, peace, freedom, have to follow the advice of your friend, President José Manuel Barroso, that we should appeal to the European Court of Human Rights for redress? Has Ireland come to this under your leadership?

How could you have so lost touch with real life, a Thaoisigh? Have you faded into the fantasy world of Hans Christian Andersen's Emperor's Clothes where the Emperor has become so enchanted with himself that no one around him will challenge him on anything – even the most blatantly illogical? In this foolishness even a non-existent cloth will make a Louis Copeland suit for the Emperor. All in Cabinet and St. Luke's concur. Only a little child full of innocence and common sense calls out the obvious *Look at the Emperor. He's as naked as the day that he was born*. What hope for Ireland, a Thaoisigh, when one of Dermot Ahern's tsunamis has whisked The Green Party and a clatter of independents into the same fantasy world.

How different for S., D. and us and all of the other 1.053 million families in this State. Even with a Celtic Tiger, we live in reality not fantasy. Our lives are real. Our horrors are real. Our threats are real. We are real. All 1.053 million families of us are real. S. is real. D. is real. We have no Celia nor even Alice to lead us through Wonderland to meet such amazing and generous characters as smiling Michael Wall and Paddy the Plasterer and the Cheshire Cat and Tweedledum and Tweedledee. No, a Thaoisigh, it must be the other way round. You need to come into our world of reality, of living, of Bunreacht na hÉireann, of action, of protection and then of happy ever after.

This is a letter of love, a Thaoisigh. Christ enjoined us to love our neighbour as ourselves and we do. But love is comparative. Christ himself told us this in his own words *Greater love has no one* (Jn 15.13). And his love for all could encompass the harshest of words for those who would harm children, for hypocrites of the law and life, for those who would not listen to reason. His love also encompassed his anger at those who would profane a sacred place with money. Christ recognised what every mother and father knows by instinct – as you too have shown, a Thaoisigh – that we love our children more than ourselves. It is a very special love that transcends not just ourselves but our neighbour. A Thaoisigh, it is not that we love you less but that we love S. and D. more.

And so we re-echo our words of a year ago to you. If you think we are in anyway unfair or too harsh, please tell us how and why. If not, please tell us why you and every member of your Government including the Minister of State for Children and Uachtarán na hÉireann have consistently chosen contrary to Bunreacht na hÉireann and every iota of human rights and natural justice to slap us down in your complicity? Remember Christ's question to the temple guard who slapped him in the face *If I did something wrong, testify as to what is wrong. But if I spoke the truth, why did you strike me* (Jn 18.23). Why have you, a Thaoisigh, and why has all your Cabinet and Uachtarán na hÉireann chosen to be a temple guard to S. to D. and to all of our family, slapping us down at every turn?

Put simply, we do not believe or accept that any legal system should oblige any mother to hand over her daughter to anyone who is abusing her child. We do not believe or accept that any social system should oblige any mother to hand over her daughter to anyone who is abusing her child. We do not believe or accept that any Government should oblige any mother to hand over her daughter to anyone who is abusing her child. Do you, a Thaoisigh?

All S. requires is the love and care and protection that is natural to any six-year-old girl. These are so basic that they pre-date Bunreacht na hÉireann and The Universal Declaration of Human Rights by thousands and thousands of years. It is because they are so basic that they are enshrined in Bunreacht na hÉireann and in The

Universal Declaration of Human Rights. Why do you choose to deny these basics to her and frustrate her mother's and our efforts to provide them?

For a combined total of one hundred and twenty-eight years we both have consistently and totally fulfilled our duty to this State as set out in Article 9.2 of Bunreacht na hÉireann:

Fidelity to the nation and loyalty to the State are fundamental political duties of all citizens.	*Is bundualgas polaitiúil ar gach saoránach bheith dílis don náisiún agus tairiseach don Stát.*

In return we look to you, now in your third term as Taoiseach, for the protection that is our right and that we deserve, for the positive response you are well capable of and for the application and consolidation of our rights as set out in this letter and in particular in Article 41.1° and 2° of Bunreacht na hÉireann:

The Family.	**An Teaghlach.**
The State recognises the Family as the natural primary and fundamental unit group of Society, and as a moral institution possessing inalienable and imprescriptible rights, antecedent and superior to all positive law.	*Admhaíonn an Stát gurb é an Teaghlach is buíon-aonad príomha bunaidh don chomhdhaonnacht de réir nádúir, agus gur foras morálta é ag a bhfuil cearta doshannta dochloíte is ársa agus is airde ná aon reacht daonna.*
The State, therefore, guarantees to protect the Family in its constitution and authority, as the necessary basis of social order and as indispensable to the welfare of the Nation and the State.	*Ós é an Teaghlach is fotha riachtanach don ord chomhdhaonnach agus ós éigeantach é do leas an Náisiúin agus an Stáit, ráthaíonn an Stát comhshuíomh agus údarás an Teaghlaigh a chaomhnú.*

In those celebrated words, slightly adapted, of Charles de Gaulle, a Thaoisigh, *L'etait c'est toi.*

Please now act immediately in relation to S., D. and all our Teaghlach and in accordance with Bunreacht na hÉireann, protect us from the unspeakable. As have each and every one of the 1.053 million families in this State, we have a God-given right to love and protect our Teaghlach – all members thereof – and the State recognises and guarantees this right in Bunreacht na hÉireann. In guaranteeing that right the State pledges and places its duty above all human laws. It is for you, a Thaoisigh, in duty and under Bunreacht na hÉireann to deliver that guarantee of protection to S., D. and to us – and to each and every one of the 1.053 million families in this State.

Faoi bhuairt is faoi bhris go fóill.

Máire agus Seán Ó L........
Taoisigh Theaghlach Uí L........

Enclosures
1. Notes to the Government of Ireland and the European Union, including Request to the Government of Ireland and the European Union, dated 27 Meán Fomhair 2005.
2. Comments so relevant to our case, 14.11.2005, presented to An Taoiseach, all members of Government, Minister of State for Children and Uachtarán na hÉireann.
3. Christmas Card 2005 sent to An Taoiseach, every member of Government, Minister of State for Children and Uachtarán na hÉireannn – Bertie Ahern, Mary Harney, Brian Cowan, Noel Dempsey, Dermot Ahern, John O'Donoghue, Micheál Ó Máirtín, Séamus Brennan, Michael McDowell, Martin Cullen, Éamon Ó Cuív, Mary Coughlan, Mary Hanafin, Willie O'Dea, Dick Roche, Brian Lenihan and Mary McAleese – at their office and their home. No one replied, not even a Christmas card.

Notes to the Government of Ireland and the European Union
1. Being legal is not necessarily being right.
2. There is no law made by Man that Man cannot change.
3. *All that is necessary for evil to succeed is that good men do nothing* (Edmund Burke).
4. Since last February we have kept the Department of Foreign Affairs fully informed of the plight and developments engulfing our daughter and grand-daughter in Sydney and our family in Sydney and Dublin.
5. The man involved is
   a. a sexual deviant, a liar, a cheat, a tax evader, a man unscrupulous in his thoughts and actions and with no respect for truth or oath
   b. a man of property
   c. ready and willing to use his trade as a cover to gain entry into people's homes.

   Activities and more to which he has admitted and which have been accepted in evidence in Court.

   In addition this man has

   d. shown no good interest in S. (even on her conception his first comment was *There are options*) until his secret life was discovered.
   e. refused to contribute even a dollar for milk or nappies on her last visit to Ireland (February-May 2003) even though he owns three properties, has invested over $1 million (tax evaded?) in a motor sports company and was awash with ready cash on the day of their departure.
   f. taken her to his bed and slept with her through the night in February he returned from riding (ostensibly on a cycling trip) through Tasmania over the charms of at least six women with such delectable appellations as Hot & Honey/Sparkleunicorn/ Tracey Tassi, and at a time when the Chief Executive Officer of New South Wales Health Authority was launching a million dollar advertising campaign against an *epidemic of sexually transmitted diseases in New South Wales*. Utterly in keeping with

his conduct, the linen on his bed had not been changed since November and was not until 25 March (Good Friday).
   g. Utterly reneged on an officially mediated separation agreement.

As pertains to any deviant he craves control over D. and S. and he is using the law to apply and maintain that control.

6. Yet on his sole word, fully supported by the Government of Ireland and the European Commission, this man could threaten our daughter with Australia's Airport Stop for months and then have his request sanctioned by the Court thus entrapping our grand-daughter and daughter (no legal semantics here, please, what entraps our grand-daughter naturally and inexorably entraps our daughter, vide the earliest and greatest judgement in a child case, I Kings 3.16-28). And so 48,000 police officers both men and women in Australia became prison wardens to a three year old child and her mother, two innocent victims of the deviant behaviour of this man who while so effectively entrapping them retains his own rights and freedom to come and go out of Australia, to visit Ireland and any country he wishes throughout the European Union and to pass with impunity through customs with any sexual infection/disease which he is currently carrying. What terrorist has 48,000 police officers personally assigned to him/her? What innocent three year old has the sins of any terrorist so unjustly assigned to him/her? What terrorist would then be given such freedom? This is not democracy. It is utter tyranny. And is fully supported and sanctioned by both the Government of Ireland and the European Union.

7. He initiated this order at less than fourteen hours notice involving us in a questionable legal system from a Legal Aid service which we discovered within those fourteen hours had corrupted (its word not ours) itself and therefore was not available to us, to the most recent judgement (our seventh visit to Court) denying our daughter permission to travel with S. to a family wedding in Ireland delivered on the side of caution! What a disgrace that no such consideration of caution has been shown to the health, body or social and moral welfare of a three year old – now four year old

– girl, to her mother, to us and to her immediate and extended family and friends.

Included along the way was the judgement that this man should have unsupervised access to this young girl twice weekly including overnight every Saturday to Sunday. This judgement *inter alia* ignored the direct conflict of evidence between the written affidavit of the man presented in Court that morning and the sworn testimony of three witnesses of his and of equally flawed character but went on to deliver judgement of such access on two grounds

- a) that the Court could not accept that the matters complained of could have happened in a public place in the light of day. Such nonsensical logicality was stood on its head some ten days later when within a couple of hundred yards of the Court a teenager (seventeen) was stabbed to death in an amusement arcade at 3.00/4.00 o'clock in the afternoon. No doubt the Honourable Judge could assuage the grief of the young man's parents with her logic and deliver the young man back to them Lazarus-like the following morning.
- b) that the Court could see no risk to the child. What Court would order that any child should overnight with any parent in a place of infection even a hospital with an MRSA environment? Indeed, what kind of parent would accept such an order?

8. On the double hearing in relation to an explicit disclosure by S. when at the first hearing the Judicial Registrar appointed a child's representative (a lawyer of the court) to represent S., ordered that all papers to date should be made available by both sides to her within forty-eight hours and gave the child's representative four weeks to report back to Court, we thought we had finally made a breakthrough. First serious doubts surfaced a week or so later when D. sought a relevant report from DOCS (Department of Child Services) and was told that she couldn't have it as it was subpoenaed by the child's representative for 8 September (for Court on 22 August!). Doubts grew alarmingly as over two and a half weeks of the four passed without any contact from the child's

representative to D. and S. Following enquiry by our solicitor such contact was made and an appointment set up for Friday 19 August (the last working day before the Court). The meeting lasted at the outside 30 minutes. At no time did the child's representative raise any matter central to the case not even to enquire about such basics as S.'s health or welfare or how they were both surviving or even their housing conditions. On the morning of the Court, before the Court opened when the child's representative heard that it was proposed to apply for permission for D. and S. to come to Ireland for a family wedding she immediately said that if that was raised in Court she would oppose it. So it wasn't.

The case wasn't called until after lunch. When it was, the child's representative immediately stood up and requested a brief adjournment because she hadn't finished reading the papers. Such was granted. When she returned, the Judicial Registrar announced he was taking a short break as he hadn't finished reading the papers either. When the Court resumed the child's representative – the Court's appointed lawyer for S. – then stood up and said that she saw no reason why contact should not continue with the child. That was the end of the matter. The Court so ruled. What tragic quasiness.

9. Our daughter has lived with the horror of this situation since May 2004 and with the terrorism of it since February 2005. So have we, as parents and grandparents, and all of our family and friends. How our daughter and ourselves have lived through so far we are at a loss to comprehend. We are also at a loss to comprehend the inaction of the Minister and Department of Foreign Affairs in our case since February, having been kept fully informed on a continuing and developing basis including our most recent meeting all of four weeks ago today and to which, our subsequent telephone calls, we have yet to receive a reply. We do not have four week periods to procrastinate and survive without some light at the end of this ever-darkening tunnel. Where is duty of care here?

10. S.'s freedom has been taken away from her and her mother (and we their family all share in the consequences) by the sins of one

man supported by the full weight of the legal system of Australia, of the Government of Ireland and of the European Union. What an utterly appalling blight and shame on the good name of Australia. What an even greater and more appalling shame on the Government of Ireland and the European Union.

Burma/Myanmar has been rightly condemned worldwide for the house arrest of Aung San Suu Kyi (whom we greatly admire). However lame, the Government of Burma/Myanmar has two excuses: Aung San Suu Kyi is an adult and she apposes Government policy. Australia, much less the Government of Ireland and the European Union, have no such excuses however lame.

11. In the unreality of the reality of any hostage situation – believe us S. and D. are hostages and so are we – it is as though officialdom is standing waiting indeed facilitating the rape of this girl. Is this what our society has fallen to – that S. and we must suffer such before anyone will move to help? Is this what the freedom that our mothers and fathers fought and prayed for has come to? Is this what the much-vaunted democracy of the European Union really means? And should the worst happen who will be held accountable – the Attorney General of Australia, the Government of Ireland, the European Union? Who will restore her innocence to this four year old and erase her mother's and our horror? Why should there be need for restoration? Whatever happened to prevention being better than cure?

12. Smiling and looking aggrieved as his sins are presented in Court he is the epitome of evil as described by Shakespeare *that one may smile and smile and be a villain*. Why shouldn't he smile as the Court facilitates his every move from initiation to completion of process, including a full year to psychologically indoctrinate (what terrorism) a three – now four year old girl that he had little or no time for prior to his unmasking with such wonderful expressions of love as *I don't like you, Mummy; I hate you, Mummy; I don't like you, Daideo; I hate you, Daideo; Daddy doesn't like you living in our new house*; to the most recent and worst of all *Who is my Mummy?*

As he imposes the new woman in his home and in his bed on this innocent child with all the concomitant threats and terror that holds for the innocent mother who has loved and cared for her daughter by the hour and by the second not only since she was born but since she was conceived (*"There are options"*). And all of this is supported fully by the Government of Ireland and the European Union. Whatever happened to duty of care, that basic duty that President Bush has had to re-find so immeasurably in the wake of hurricane Katrina and is now showing in abundance through the reality of hurricane Rita? Is it too much to ask for our grand-daughter, our daughter, our family and ourselves that the Government of Ireland and the European Union would both take a moment to find their duty of care to us and to offer the support we request?

13. After seven visits to Court there is nothing in the Australian legal system to give us – not just D. and S. but all of our family – hope of anything but a minimum fourteen years sentence and continuance, most likely worsening, of the terror and horror we now endure.
14. We are lifelong (60 & 65 years respectively) law-abiding citizens of Ireland and of Europe, law-abiding citizens of the European Union since Ireland's accession on 1 January 1973, members of one of the oldest families in Ireland and so of one of the oldest families in Europe. We respectfully and urgently ask the Government of Ireland to act on our Requests of 30 August and seek the support of the European Union for these Requests which we hereby present for immediate action also by the European Union (*vide* attached page).

Signed: ....
Máire agus Seán Ó L........   Date: 27 Meán Fómhair 2005

N.B. These notes are only a précis of some that has happened to date. We will happily answer any question arising – asked urgently to facilitate urgent action – or on any other events to date.

A Thaoisigh

Requests to the Government of Ireland and the European Union
1. That D. and S. be brought home immediately to Ireland, that S. be given an Irish and European Union passport (for which a duly completed application even if out of date exists – and why should it be considered out of date in this case?). and that any outstanding matters legal or otherwise be finalised in Ireland.
2. That the Government of Ireland and the European Union be responsible for providing any resources needed in this case, including finance, legal services, health-care, action programme and due diligence and any and all services required to achieve 1 above.
3. That the Government of Ireland and the European Union provide comprehensive information to Irish and European citizens going to Australia – all the more urgently relevant now that Australia is seeking to attract 25,000 citizens from Ireland and the U.K. to re-locate to Australia.
4. That the Government of Ireland and the European Union will provide a system and resources to aid Irish and European citizens who find themselves in trouble overseas.

Signed: ....
Máire agus Seán Ó L……..   Date: 27 Meán Fómhair 2005

Comments so relevant to our case, 14.11.2005, presented to An Taoiseach, all members of Government, Minister of State for Children and Uachtarán na hÉireann.

1. *Horrendous.* Bishop David Cremin, Sydney, in relation to our case, February 2005.
2. A spokesman for Mr. Ahern said he was willing to do anything that would be seen as helpful (re Rory Carroll, Irish Times, 20.10.2005).
3. *Last night we were in the depths of despondency.* Joe Carroll, 21.10.2005.
4. . . . . the responses of those in authority to these criminal acts was wholly inadequate. Irish Times editorial 26.10.2005.
5. Dr. Walsh has been stringent in insisting on the paramount safety of children. Irish Times, 26.10.2005.
6. Where an organization is aware of a serious problem within its structure with criminal and child protection implications, it has a duty to alert and inform its personnel of this and to ensure that every step is taken to eliminate it as soon as possible. The Ferns Report.
7. Those who wantonly or recklessly engage in conduct that creates a substantial risk of sexual abuse to a child should be prosecuted for reckless endangerment, The Ferns Report.
8. *We will act on all these matters speedily.* An Taoiseach, Bertie Ahern, Dáil Éireann 25.10.2005.
9. *Child Protection is not a discretionary issue.* Brian Lenihan, Minister of State for Children, 25.10.2005.
10. *We cannot have employers, or bishops, or anyone else say that their own internal work rules, or canon law, prevent them from taking action. ibid.*
11. *On behalf of the Government I want to condemn in the strongest possible terms the repeated failure and gross dereliction of duties of those in positions of trust . . . who failed to take effective steps to defend and vindicate the rights of the children concerned. ibid.*
12. *The enquiry concluded that there is a good practice in Ferns. I want to see that happen everywhere else. ibid.*

13. *We must learn from mistakes of the past.* ibid.
14. *In addition to increasing public awareness and understanding of the horror of child sexual abuse, this report provides practical and far-reaching recommendations to ensure a speedy and effective response to reports of abuse.* ibid.
15. *The Government also favours the creation of new powers . . . to bar any person from being with children if there were reasonable grounds for believing they were capable of abuse.* ibid.
16. *It is now clear that many children would not have suffered abuse had those with knowledge acted on it.* Dr. Diarmuid Martin, 25.10.2005.
17. *The betrayal of trust is horrendous.* Dr. Seán Brady, 25.10.2005.
18. *I am appalled and overwhelmed at the nature and extent of the abuse.* An Taoiseach, Bertie Ahern, 25.10.2005.
19. Minister for Justice Michael McDowell said he would introduce amendments to the current Criminal Justice Bill to reflect one of the key recommendations in the report, advising that a law on *reckless endangerment* should be considered. The law would make it a criminal offence for professionals to fail to take action to protect children if they become aware of a potential risk from sexual or physical abuse. Irish Times, 26.10.2005.
20. *The Government will not take at face value what the Church says about sexual abuse.* Michael McDowell, Minister for Justice, 28.10.2005.
21. *I asked the Bishops to cooperate fully both individually and collectively with the recommendations of the report.* Brian Lenihan, Minister of State for Children, 28.10.2005.
22. *. . . where this abuse has existed it must be cleared out once and for all and be dealt with.* An Taoiseach, Bertie Ahern, Dáil Éireann, 26.10.2005.
23. *You can never be too cautious when it comes to complaints of child sex abuse and children have to be believed and children have to be listened to.* An Tánaiste and Minister for Health, Mary Harney, 26.10.2005.
24. *And clearly we need new provisions in our criminal justice legislation to make it a criminal offence for anybody to protect a child abuser and*

25. *that will be done by the Minister for Justice in legislation that is currently before the Oireachtas. ibid.*
26. *Let us see some initiative in the next budget and let us see something that really deals with the issue, that looks after families . . . and that looks after Irish society.* Senator Margaret Cox, Seanad Éireann. 26.10.2005.
26. *Mr. McDowell will bring proposals to set up such an inquiry to the Cabinet as a matter of urgency.* Brian Lenihan, Minister of State for Children.
27. *It made it very clear that the church regarded itself as in a position not to reveal to the civil authorities what was going on in a way that most of us now would regard as completely unacceptable.* Michael McDowell, Minister for Justice, 27.10.2005.
28. *Nobody should be debarred from seeking justice for want of finances.* Michael McDowell, Minister for Justice, 28.10.2005.
29. *The law treats sexual assaults on children as serious crimes, and an adult perpetrator is normally considered fully responsible for his actions.* Irish Times, 28.10.2005.
30. *In the end, we will remember not the words of our enemies but the silence of our friends.* Martin Luther King Jr.
31. *It is easy to say this happened because the Catholic Church and the State masked the stench with sweet perfumes, took a deep breath and savoured the clear, clean air.* Fintan O'Toole, Irish Times, 29.10.2005.
32. *The Ferns Report illustrates not only the Catholic Church's callous indifference to the welfare of children, but also the culpability of the State and the wider public. ibid.*
33. *The church's response to child abuse was collusive and the State's utterly negligent. ibid.*
34. *I think if it had been my child, I'd be serving time at this stage.* Senator Joe O'Toole, Seanad Éireann, 29.10.2005.
35. *I am unable to attempt to describe the mental and emotional state of a child or teenager sexually abused by a priest or the loneliness of carrying such a harrowing secret through the growing up years and into adulthood.* Bishop Eamonn Walsh, 30.10.2005.

36. He removed her boots, trousers and underwear and attempted to place his hands between her legs. For this sexual assault on a 10-year-old girl, James Lombard (37) was jailed for seven years in Cork Criminal Court, 4.11.2005.
37. *We in the Roman Catholic Church must surely ask why such evil continued to go unchecked for so long.* Bishop Willie Walsh, 6.11.2005.
38. When trust is eroded, societies implode. It would be well for politicians and journalists alike to tread a bit more carefully in their response to clerical abuse scandals. Professor Fr. Vincent Twomey, 8.11.2005.
39. Anyone in a position of trust must show that they are people of character and integrity. *ibid.*
40. *. . . we are the first generation to have within our reach the great destination of our egalitarian Republic where the strong are driven by the restless and unselfish duty of care for the weak, and where every life is given the chance to fully blossom.* President Mary McAleese, keynote speech, Filling the Vacuum conference, Co. Clare, 7.11.2005.
41. The Irish people will never settle for what she termed *Destination Complacency*, President Mary McAleese, Irish Times, 8.11.2005.
42. *Cases of this nature are horrific for victims of sexual abuse and this case is not different in the horror it inflicted on this young girl* (4-5 years-old). Judge Donagh McDonagh, Dublin Criminal Court, 10.11.2005.
43. *I have full power to notify certain things to the commission.* Brian Lenihan, Minister of State for Children, 8.11.2005.
44. The perniciousness of the denial mechanism is that it can pervade all areas of community life. The instinct to defend the established moral authority within the land has resulted in an unwillingness to believe and defend the victims of all kinds of abuse. Mary Raftery, Irish Times, 10.11.2005.
45. It is of vital importance for us as a society to expose and root out this propensity for denial and the enormous damage that it causes. *ibid.*

46. The victims, their families, the wider community of faith are angry too and are entitled to question and critique in the face of silence and footdragging. Irish Catholic editorial, 27.10.2005.
47. Bishops have erred, priests have fallen, and no amount of apologies or compensation can give back what was taken from innocent children. *ibid*, 3.11.2005.
48. I am writing as one who suffered sexual abuse in childhood, beginning at age four . . . It is extremely difficult to recover from the terrible and complex psychic injuries inflicted by abuse endured in one's tender and vulnerable years . . . Hearing the horrifying stories contained in the Ferns Report, can reawaken most painfully the trauma of all those who struggle with a legacy of sexual abuse in childhood . . . as well as the behaviour of those in positions of responsibility who failed to take action and, indeed, covered up crime. A priest victim, another S., Irish Catholic, 3.11.2005.
49. *The emergence of truth, however painful, must always be beneficial. I believe that these painful truths which have emerged will have a cleansing effect on all our institutions.* Bishop Willie Walsh, 6.11.2005.
50. *All of this is so true and so horrendous but I am still not impressed with the juggling of apologies and generalities . . . These people (sexual deviants) are brilliant and so devious. As 'outsiders' most of us cannot even begin to grasp the mind-set of their 'connivance'. If we attempt to work on the words 'Denial and enable' then we grasp a little of the difficulty. Plausibility and grandiosity are decorated with lies . . . They are like 'terrorists' everywhere. They beat us every time. And these are terrorists . . . They can undermine our way of life. They can spread disease everywhere. This is not an issue of blame, but rather an insight into deviant behaviour.* Fr. Seamus Ahearne, 10.11.2005.
51. *Our thoughts go out to the victims and their families.* An Taoiseach, Bertie Ahern, Dáil Éireann, 25.10.2005.
52. *Sexual abuse of children is a horrendous crime.* Bishop Michael Neary, 27.10.2005.
53. One of the greatest cruelties committed against children in the

Diocese of Ferns was the cruelty of silence. We have seen the evidence of the damage such silence causes and we must ensure that we never again allow such silence to exist. Irish Society of the Prevention of Cruelty to Children, 25.10.2005.
54. *When you read such a litany of horrible, horrible gross abuse and rape, it leaves you speechless.* Bishop Éamonn Walsh, 24.10.2005.
55. Judge Murphy does not exaggerate when he portrays the many victims who helped his enquiry as heroic. Irish Independent 29.10.2005.
56. *It's very sad when young people are hurt in any way – and our first response has to be to those who suffered the abuse. We have to try to reach out to them in every way. That is our primary objective, the protection of children. We have to offer them a full and sympathetic hearing.* Bishop John Buckley, 28.10.2005
57. *Obviously the Ferns report is – the extent of it, the numbers involved, the plight of young people, boys and girls – truly shocking. There is no doubt about that.* An Taoiseach, Bertie Ahern, Sunday Tribune, 30.10.2005.
58. *. . . the horrendous hurt of victims of sexual abuse.* An Taoiseach, Bertie Ahern, lunch for European Journalists.
59. A man suffered chronic post-traumatic stress disorder after he was sexually abused as a child . . . it was about lost innocence, lost childhood, and a life spent in rage. Forty years later, his client was still suffering . . . He said that in the course of teaching Feeney would sit beside him in his desk and fondle his genitals . . . As a child he had difficulties passing water and felt the pains he was getting then were because of what Feeney did . . . He later lost a kidney. Report of High Court case, Irish Times, 10.11.2005.
60. The Government's plan to offer presidential pardons to IRA fugitives . . . up to 100 so called "on the runs" . . . cannot be challenged. The pardons . . . will be awarded by President Mary McAleese under Article 13.6 of the Constitution. Irish Times 11.11.2005.
61. *Horrendous.* Bishop David Cremin, Sydney, in relation to our case, February 2005.

Christmas Card 2005

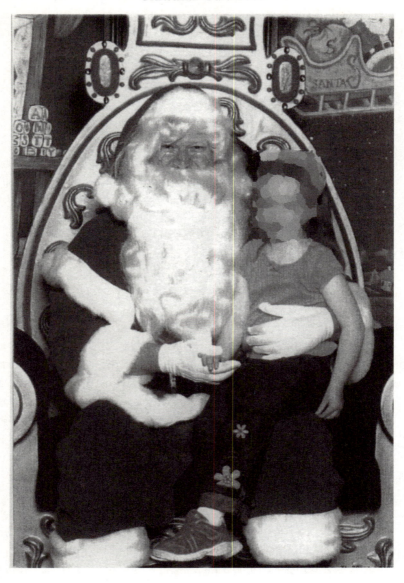

*Ny name is S.
I wish you Nollaig Shona*

My name is S. I'm four. My mummy cries. I don't like it when she cries. Nor when Mamó and Daideo are sad. My daddy plays with me and I don't like it. He does things to me. As a big government person, you let him. Just talk to Bertie and Dermot they've known all about me for months and months. Like the Bishops they've chosen to do nothing, thinking they can hide.

My mummy has to hand me over to daddy on Christmas Eve morning. Please think of me for Christmas. I'll be back safe with Mummy on Christmas Day at 5.00p.m. Until Tuesday, the eve of the Holy Innocents. Mummy says I'm one of them.

I'm S. I'm four. Please help me and mummy. Please talk to Bertie and Dermot because you're all in this together. My angel guardian says it's called complicity. And what's happening to me is called abuse.

Nollaig Shona le grá to you and your family, particularly if you've got a little girl like me. I'm four. My name is S. What I do not have – Freedom, is all mummy and I want for Christmas and the New Year and always.

Let the little children alone – Jesus Christ

The horrendous hurt of victims of sexual abuse/I am appalled and overshelmed at the nature and extent of the abuse/where this abuse has existed it must be cleared out once and for all and be dealt with/we will act on all these matters speedily – An Taoiseach

Child protection is not a discretionary issue – Minister of State for Children

Sexual abuse of children is a horrendous crime – Archbishop of Tuam

Cases of this nature are horrific for victims of sexual abuse and this case is not different in the horror it inflicted on this young girl (4-5 years old) – Dublin Criminal Court

Nobody should be debarred from seeking justice for want of finance – Minister for Justice

Ráthaíonn an Stát gan cur isteach lena dhlithe ar chearta pearsanta aon saoránaigh, agus ráthaíonn fós na cearta sin a chosaint is a shuíomh lena dhlithe sa mhéid gur féidir é – Bunreacht na hÉireann

Admhaíonn an Stát gurb é an Teaghlach is buíon-aonad príomha bunaidh don chomhdhaonnacht de réir nádúir, agus gur foras morálta é ag a bhfuil cearta doshannta dochloite is ársa agus is airde ná aon reacht daonna. Ós é an Teaghlach is fotha riachtanach don ord chomhdhaonnach agus ós éigeantach é do leas an Náisiúin agus an Stáit, ráthaíonn an Stát comhshuíomh agus údarás an Teaghlaigh a chaomhnú – Bunreacht na hÉireann

our egalitarian Republic where the strong are driven by the restless and unselfish duty of care for the weak and where every life is given the chance to blossom – Uachtarán na hÉireann

Any law which transfers the guilt of a forty-something man to an innocent woman and a three year old girl and takes away their freedom is not democracy: it is utter tyranny – mo Dhaideo.